Quantity

AND

Quality

SANDRA
WILDE

Increasing the **Volume** *and* **Complexity** *of Students' Reading*

HEINEMANN
Portsmouth, NH

Heinemann

361 Hanover Street

Portsmouth, NH 03801–3912

www.heinemann.com

Offices and agents throughout the world

© 2013 by Sandra Wilde

Library of Congress Cataloging-in-Publication Data
Wilde, Sandra.
    Quantity and quality : increasing the volume and complexity of students' reading / Sandra Wilde. — First edition.
        pages cm
    Includes bibliographical references.
    ISBN 978-0-325-04796-6
    1. Reading—United States. 2. Language arts—Standards—United States. 3. English language—Study and teaching—Standards—United States.   I. Title.
LB1050.W4384 2013
428.4—dc23   2013020664

Editor: Tina Miller
Production: Patty Adams
Cover and interior designs: Suzanne Heiser
Cover image: Neal Lankester/Alamy
Typesetter: Eric Rosenbloom, Kirby Mountain Composition
Manufacturing: Steve Bernier

Printed in the United States of America on acid-free paper
17 16 15 14 13 EBM 1 2 3 4 5

CONTENTS

ACKNOWLEDGMENTS

I've so appreciated working again with my brilliant editor and friend Tina Miller at Heinemann, who always has great suggestions and a fresh eye, and believes deeply in my work. Kate Montgomery helped me sharpen the focus of the book in a couple of long phone conversations, as well as by reading parts of the manuscript. Debra Doorack also gave the manuscript an intelligent reading.

I'm again very happy to work again with talented production editor Patty Adams, who's happy to answer my most neurotic questions and really gets what I'm trying to do in my writing. I've also again benefited from the services of copyeditor David Cottingham, an author's dream, who catches all the little things I've missed but leaves my style alone.

Eric Chalek, marketing manager, came up with the perfect title after we'd all played around with not-quite-right ones for months. He also understands what the book is about and how to communicate it to potential readers. Suzanne Heiser, design manager, created a cover that is brilliant both literally and figuratively, even kindly including some specific colors that I liked.

At Hunter College, City University of New York, I'd like to especially thank Genevieve Joseph, Jade Michaels, Hazera Jalil, and Angela Calvo, for their dedication, helpfulness, and pleasantness.

At PS/IS 180, Hugo Newman Preparatory School in New York, principal Peter McFarlane has welcomed me into his school since 2004, four years before I moved to New York. Special thanks, of course, to dedicatees Carolyn Montalto and her 2012–13 class. Liz Eck and a number of other teachers have also invited me into their classrooms.

In my neighborhood, shout-outs to the super of my building, Marcin Korzep, and lobby attendants Robert Morris, James New, and Emir Gonzales, as well as

Mohammed Touray (proprietor of All Things Variety Store). A special word of thanks to Sgt. Keisha Ward of NYPD.

Thanks to a good friend, Jane Bean-Folkes of Rowan University, who is always happy to talk at length about literacy. Thanks also to Stephen Krashen and Richard Allington, whose work has deeply informed the writing of this book, and a tip of the hat to the late Jeanette Veatch, who I met in 1978 and whose work from half a century ago still provides a clear foundational vision for helping kids learn to read.

The dedication of this book reflects my experiences with reading from my earliest years to today. My late mother, Anita Axelson, got me reading before I started school, not by teaching but by getting me into the books that we always had at home. She read to me, took me to the library, sometimes complained that I had my nose in a book too much, but supported my life as a voracious reader, whether it was comic books, classics, all the Oz books, or even movie magazines.

I develop many of my present and future thoughts about reading in the classroom of Carolyn Montalto through her and the sixth-grade students I've worked with this year: Amadou, Brandon, Brianni, Chantell, Daniel, Darrein, Destiny, Elijah, Elijah, Emad, Enrique, Hulematou, Jonathan, Joshua, Julio, Karina, Khadijah, Koyan, Langa, Malakai, Malcolm, Princess, Sanaa, Shiva, Sumona, Thierno, and Trevon. I'm constantly amazed by their love of reading, their willingness to push themselves, and especially their intellectuality. These kids never heard an idea they didn't want to talk about. Special thanks to the nonfiction group, who accepted my challenge to push themselves into harder nonfiction. It's not true that kids only want to read books on topics they're already interested in: they snapped up books on fish extinction, world architecture, and World War II, as well as the more obvious favorites about sports, dance, and Navy Seals. Carolyn was gracious and fun in encouraging me to pursue whatever ideas the kids and I felt like exploring, including a small group exploring Middle English and verb tenses, and a trip to a dark room to debunk the "Bloody Mary" hex. So much thanks to Carolyn and the kids, and keep up the good work.

PART ONE

Why?

CHAPTER 1

Volume and Complexity

The premise of this book is simple: that establishing the reading of books as the center of our literacy curriculum is the secret to academic achievement. Students from grades 1 to 12 need to read more books than they do now, and to gradually move into harder books. This isn't mere recreational reading, nor is it requiring them to read "grade-level" books. It's getting kids reading, and making sure that readers are growing.

The core principles are the following:

1. Everyone reads a lot, including setting personal goals, as described below.

2. Everyone reads widely: fiction and information, different genres, topics, and styles. You can also read narrowly or deeply if you want: all of the *Twilight* books in a row, everything you can find on spiders.

3. Everyone grows as a reader. The goal each year is to read more challenging books over the course of the year than those you read at the beginning. The reader chooses the books, but the teacher mentors.

4. There's time for reading during the school day. The amount will vary depending on circumstances, but reading needs to be part of school, not just a hobby.

5. Teachers help kids become smarter readers. This includes literal and informational understanding, and also literary appreciation. There needs to be plenty

of teaching, in individual conferences and in lessons and conversations for small groups and the whole class.

6. Everyone keeps a record of books read. Readers need to monitor and document the extent of their reading.

These twelve years in school are the beginning of each student's whole life as a reader. It's not just about learning to read because they'll need it for college and career; it's about becoming a reader as part of who they are right now and for whatever they do in their personal and professional lives in the decades ahead.

Volume, range, growth, time, sophistication, documenting, ownership for life. That's it.

I'm suggesting—no, shouting—that there can be nothing more important than putting reading at the very center of what goes on in your classroom. This is especially true in the self-contained classrooms of elementary schools and many middle schools, but also applies in somewhat different ways to the departmentalized programs of secondary schools. One very important reason for focusing on reading so forcefully is that these are the years when students have the time to read: indeed, the learning that it represents is their primary job. When they get to college, their learning will be much more narrowly focused, and adult life in the family and workplace will be even busier. They need to leave each grade, up through the end of high school, with a solid foundation of books read, and the ability to read harder books than they could at the beginning.

Notice that I'm focusing on books; written language is available in many other forms today, and the pull of screens is strong, but readers need the length and weight of books for the depth and complexity of learning and feeling they provide. A short story, no matter how great, will never stay with you the way a novel does. You'll learn only a small amount about Martin Luther King from a blog post, as compared to a biography. The ether is alive with millions of snippets of ideas, but extended experiences with ideas and stories in books are the solid foundation of reading and learning.

We have clear and abundant evidence that reading a lot matters. It's not enough to teach students how to read, we have to ensure that they *do* read. Listed below are ten big ideas to make my case. Although in a sense they're statements about the value of reading in general, their real power comes when the volume read is large and the complexity of what's read increases over time. (I owe a great debt here to the work of Stephen D. Krashen, whose *Power of Reading* [2004] provides a comprehensive, book-length account of research supporting the idea that reading itself, and lots of it, supports students' learning in many ways. His work underlies all ten of these big ideas. He also makes clear what adults need to do to allow this reading to happen, beginning with the most basic: access to books.)

1. There's a strong, strong connection between how much students have read and their reading achievement.

The table on page 12 (Anderson, Wilson, and Fielding, 1988) shows the relationship between the time that students read per day and their level of proficiency. This isn't surprising. The cultural observer Malcolm Gladwell (2008) poses the idea that it takes 10,000 hours of practice to become an expert. (We're talking professional pianists, chess Grandmasters, and Bill Gates.) Ten thousand hours of reading spread throughout grades 1–12 would take two hours a day, every day of the year, which seems like a lot. But if kids read only half an hour a day, they could have read for 2,500 hours by grade 12. (Remember, the best readers are already reading an hour a day.) The authors of the books that children read are their most important reading teachers.

2. Reading makes you a better writer.

Even young children's writing reflects the kinds of reading that they've been exposed to (DeFord, 1981). The more kinds of writing you read, the more ways you'll be able to write yourself. It's not hard to write the way you talk, but it's hard to be a good writer if you're only representing speech written down; you need to know in your bones what good writing looks and sounds like, the more the better. Indeed, learning to use the special style of writing, the forms and words that rarely appear in speech, can only come from reading (Krashen, 2004, 132–34). Heck, reading a lot is even the biggest factor in how good a speller you are (Wilde, 1992).

3. Reading builds your vocabulary.

Not only does reading build your vocabulary, it's almost impossible to learn large numbers of words without it. There's a basic vocabulary of spoken English, then a wider range of words that occur less commonly in speech, then a huge universe of words that are found almost exclusively in books. We know that the words in the latter group are acquired almost entirely through reading, particularly with repeated exposure (Nagy, Herman, and Anderson, 1985).

4. Reading helps you learn.

This of course is obvious, but what I'd like to underline here is the efficiency of reading as a learning tool. The Internet is fine if you want to learn a little bit about a topic (dependent on the reliability of the website, of course), but is problematic for in-depth knowledge, because of search and reliability issues. We can find *information* quickly online, but *knowledge* is more complex. You can also get information from a video, but reading is easily twice as fast, so you can learn more. Also, you control the rate in reading, so you can speed up during parts where the content is more familiar to you. For the typical reader, an hour spent reading a book about the solar system will produce far more learning than an hour spent watching an educational video, and can be more closely tied to one's preexisting level of knowledge. Since books are edited and reviewed, the information in them has been screened for accuracy and quality of presentation in a way that Internet information may not be.

5. Reading helps you understand life better.

I'm speaking particularly about fiction and memoir here, the power of stories. Reading is a way to get inside other people's heads and understand their lives; you often learn more about them than you know about your friends. Even though fictional characters aren't real people, their authors have created them to explore human issues. Reading takes you outside the limits of your own experience, thereby helping you develop as a person.

6. Reading prepares you for all of adult life.

If you arrive at college with strong reading muscles and have experienced reading a lot of books of all kinds, you'll be well prepared for the courses you take. If you arrive in the workplace having read a lot, you'll be able to comfortably adapt to whatever literacy you need there. You'll also be able to be an intelligent citizen and consumer, able to read serious newspapers and magazines rather than being limited to tabloids. You'll also have the habits and abilities in place to be a lifelong learner; you can read books about parenting, places you're going to travel to, serious fiction — whatever you want. Personal reading in adult life need not be just a form of recreation, an alternative to TV or sports; it's not just a pastime but ideally a deep and regular source of life enrichment.

7. Volume of reading can help close the achievement gap.

Poverty can lead to a downward spiral in reading achievement. Students in poor neighborhoods are less likely to have access to books, therefore likely to read less, therefore less likely to read well. The "summer slump" in reading achieve-ment has been found to be due largely to class differences in access to books and therefore in amount read over the summer (Allington and McGill-Franzen, 2012). Lower-achieving children are more likely to be taught in ways that involve less actual reading (Allington, 1977). There's no reason why all children can't be reading the quantity and types of books that many of those from higher social classes already are.

8. Reading a lot helps the next generation.

Many children who don't read much have parents who, through no fault of their own, don't read much themselves, perhaps for reasons that go back generations. The parents, particularly of immigrants, may not be literate in English or even in their home language; indeed, their home language may not even have a written form. If we can create a generation of readers, we'll be creating a generation of parents in whose homes books are an essential part of children's upbringing.

9. Reading a lot finesses many curriculum concerns and issues.

If students are really reading more books and pushing into harder books, they'll master the Common Core State Standards, acquire much of the cultural literacy that Hirsch (1987) said was necessary for all citizens in a democracy (e.g., a passing acquaintance with terms and names like *macho*, *macrocosm*, *Madagascar*, and *maestro*), and pass standardized tests. They won't need to memorize spelling or vocabulary words. You won't need to download worksheets from the Internet or go to teacher stores. You'll be able to find a way to work in, with minimal angst, any books that your school district requires kids to read.

10. Reading is a gift to students.

I'm going to share a personal story here. I remember sitting in a reading group when I was about eight years old, being told the new words in the Dick and Jane story, and realizing that I already knew what the teacher was trying to teach me. I'd been a voracious reader since before I started school, and was almost always bored by the official reading we did in school, all the way through high school. My real intellectual life always went on in the reading I did outside of school, although it got harder and harder to fit in with each year's increasing homework pressures. Everything I've achieved in literacy, including the writing of several books, is grounded in the reading I did when younger, with the school reading largely irrelevant. (In college, when I got to choose my own courses, it got much better.) What a gift it can be to get students immersed in reading from the beginning and throughout, so that they can have an intellectual life *in* school.

I've told you why: now I'll tell you what and how. Each chapter deals with both volume and complexity; each chapter is a tool to support students' reading a lot of books and gradually reading harder books.

CHAPTER 2

How Many Books, and Why?

The first central premise of this book is that students should read a lot of books, more than most of them do already. So how much *do* they read now? First, some history and thoughts about the amount of reading in the English language arts curriculum. The amount of reading going on in classrooms and as homework was fairly limited for a long time (particularly in the era of universal basal readers), expanded with readers' workshop approaches, and shrank again with the wide use of scripted programs in the last decade. We've always had expectations for students' reading, such as reading at grade level (to be defined later), and increasingly these have come in the form of standards, most recently the Common Core State Standards, which are for all practical purposes national standards and will define the territory for years to come. For decades, as documented in *Report Card on Basal Readers* (Shannon and Goodman, 1988), elementary-school teaching of reading was defined by basal readers, typically student anthologies of short pieces, largely fiction, with accompanying teachers' manuals, lessons, workbooks, and assessments. The total quantity of reading in each elementary grade might amount to several hundred pages, as might be found in one or two thick anthologies for each grade level. Basal readers began to change around the 1980s with the addition of more nonfiction, extra materials such as short, single-topic books for extra reading, and increasingly, media, digital, and online resources. Simultaneously, many classrooms began moving away from the basal reader model to whole language and reading workshop approaches, the former promulgated through the work of the Whole Language Umbrella and the latter seen widely, for instance, in the books and professional development work produced by Lucy Calkins and her colleagues through Teachers College, Columbia University. (Nancie Atwell, 1987, was also an early originator.) Two important precursors of this approach were Jeannette Veatch (1978) beginning in the 1950s for reading workshop, and Donald Graves (1983), Calkins's mentor, for writing workshop in the 1980s. At the other end of the spectrum, in the 2000s, many schools adopted highly scripted reading programs under the influence of the National Reading Panel and Reading First initiatives, where the focus was on very structured guidance in reading relatively small amounts of text.[1]

The picture changes somewhat in the secondary grades, including middle school, where reading in the English language arts curriculum moves to a focus on literature rather than learning to read, using anthologies and complete works such as novels and plays, usually with a strong emphasis on a canon of old and newer classics, while content-area classes typically use textbooks that are often very difficult for students.

It's not easy to say definitively how much kids actually read in school, in the past and today. How much should they be reading, in and out of school? Classroom literacy practices almost certainly vary more widely now than forty years ago, although they may become more homogeneous with the Common Core State Standards, whose focus is very much on close work with grade-level texts. Because of the nature of different programs, children in readers' workshop settings are likely to read the most and those in scripted programs the least, with basal reader programs somewhere in between. (Of course, how much children read also

---

[1] Although these approaches were highly touted as definitively based on research, they were strongly critiqued (see especially Allington, 2002). Also, there were findings of corrupt practices in urging schools to implement them (www2.ed.gov/about/offices/list/oig/auditrpts/stmt042007.pdf).

includes that which they do of their own choosing, outside of school and when given time for it in the classroom. Many classrooms using formal programs also have varying amounts of free-choice reading time during the school day.) In high school, assigned reading of class texts is common, although many students may not actually read the books.

As far as I know, there have only rarely been standards for volume of reading. New York State has a 2009 English Language Arts Resource Guide for Core Curriculum with a standard of students' reading twenty-five books per year in grades preK–12 (http://emsc32.nysed.gov/ciai/ela/pub/ccela.pdf), but this isn't typical. The Common Core State Standards focus on what students should be able to do — ranging from examples like retelling familiar stories in kindergarten, comparing and contrasting the overall structure of two texts in fifth grade, and demonstrating knowledge of foundational works of American literature in eleventh and twelfth — but don't directly address volume of reading. One of the two consortia assigned to develop curriculum materials for the standards, PARCC, has developed model content frameworks. Using the sixth grade as an example, they suggest four modules over the course of a year, each one including three to five short texts and one longer one, such as a novel or a play (www.parcconline.org/sites/parcc/files/PARCCMCFforELALiteracyGRADE6_FINALAug2012.pdf). If these recommendations are used as guidelines by curriculum publishers, student reading in school may not be very wide or extensive, with close reading of only a small number of texts considered central.

Perhaps the best answers to how much students read in school and for homework are that we don't know, and that it varies a lot. But we do have suggestive data about how much kids read generally. A classic study (Anderson, Wilson, and Fielding, 1988) surveyed fifth-grade students about how much time they read outside of school, then extrapolated this data to determine how many words they read per year. This is one study, conducted a while ago, on one group of students, but I believe that its findings probably ring true for American students as a whole. It found huge differences in the amounts read by better readers and weaker ones (as measured by standardized tests).[2] I've constructed this table from the study's data. (Percentile refers to how students compare to others on a test; for instance, a student at the 90th percentile scored better than 90 percent of children taking the test.)

Percentile rank on reading tests	Minutes of book reading per day[3]	Words read per year
98	65	4,358,000
90	40	1,823,000
70	22	622,000
50	13	282,000
30	6	106,000
10	2	8,000

A book appropriate for this grade level, such as *Hatchet* by Gary Paulsen, contains about 50,000 words (Allington, 2012). The best 2 percent of readers were therefore reading the equivalent of eighty-seven books a year, the average kids about six, and the bottom 10 percent a small fraction of one. If we want all students to be strong readers, six books a year just isn't going to cut it. Also, the reading gap between those who read a lot and those who don't will increase every year until they finish high school and enter college or the workplace. That time spent not reading can only with great difficulty be made up, if at all. Therefore, Richard Allington (2012) suggests a standard of ninety minutes a day for reading in school up through sixth grade, and much more reading in high school than is currently the case. (I'll talk later about

---

[2] Incidentally, the mean amount of time spent watching television for all the students was thirteen times the amount of time spent reading books. This study was of course conducted before the majority of today's new media were common.

[3] The authors also looked at reading of other material: magazines, newspapers, comic books, and mail. The stronger the readers, the greater the proportion of their reading time was with books.

how to focus your teaching to allow this much time for reading and also to ensure that students aren't just experiencing a study hall approach to reading.)

Reading, a lot of it, has got to be the center of our reading curriculum, just like cooking is at the center of cooking school. Everything else that goes on must be in support of readers spending time constructing meaning from the books they read. Reading itself develops not only reading ability but the knowledge that comes from reading and the habits that support a lifetime of reading. Volume of reading is made up of the time spent reading and the number of books read, and for adult Americans, it's dropping. Only 57 percent of American adults had read a book in the last year when interviewed in 2002, down from 61 percent two years earlier (National Endowment for the Arts, 2007). Younger adults read less than older ones.

Let's think about the school year, with a length of thirty-five weeks. How many books per week should children be reading, once they're reading independently? There's no single answer for every classroom and every student, since books vary in length and children vary in proficiency and interest, but here are some suggestions. These are meant to be the numbers of books that children read as individuals, not read-alouds; and to go beyond—indeed, well beyond—the books you "teach" (those you spend time working on with children as a whole class or in guided-reading groups). If students are also reading at the same pace at home and during the summer, when their time is less structured, you can double the numbers for the year. It's crucial that students choose their own books to read, but they aren't limited to their own unmediated selections. The rest of this book will explore how to help children curate their choices so that they're growing in proficiency and sophistication, and realize that they're doing so. The choice and ownership are there, but the teacher's there too.

Let's start by thinking about early readers, those who are reading independently in easy-reading books and beginning chapter books: think *Frog and Toad.* Chapter 8 explores how to get children reading independently as quickly as possible, early in first grade for most. They should be able to read at least one to two of these every day in school, including repeated readings. A reasonable goal for the school year would then be around 250–300 books per child.

In the early elementary grades, children will move into short novels and easier nonfiction books, such as the *Alvin Ho* and *Ivy and Bean* books, and inexpensive paperback nonfiction books, often published in series format and widely available. Students can easily read a book a day, for a total of around 150–180 a year.

The upper elementary grades and middle school are the years for reading longer chapter books, moving into young adult books: *Moon over Manifest*, *The Hunger Games*. The lengths of books start to vary more at these grade levels, with short novels like *Hatchet* and longer ones like the Harry Potter books. Nonfiction books may be heavily illustrated, which means they can be read faster than their page lengths would suggest. How about 100 pages a week as a goal, which would lead to a yearly total of 3,500 pages for the school year, working out to a total of maybe thirty-five books? This is clearly a reasonable goal, and would place students at the 90th percentile of the children in the study mentioned above.

High school students will be reading young adult and adult fiction and nonfiction, with the latter being in addition to any textbooks for content-area classes: Walter Dean Myers, Amy Tan, James Gleick. In high school the content demands of the curriculum become more intense, but wide reading can be part of both English language arts and content classes. English classes could do fewer class books and more book groups and self-chosen reading projects. Content classes could add choice reading from text sets on topics such as World War II or animal biology. Across all classes (with some coordination so that wide reading is spread evenly throughout the year), twenty books a year (with a probable average length of about 200 pages) seems like a reasonable minimum.

These are goals for all students. English language learners should be encouraged to read books in their first language early on, and continue to after their English reading abilities improve. Special needs students will need some accommodations; a good rule of thumb is that they should be encouraged to spend as much time reading as other students, even if the amount they're able to read is less. Audio books and other technology can provide support for visually impaired students and those with reading disabilities, compensating for what they can't do as well visually while providing many of the cognitive benefits of reading.

Imagine a school system having a goal that its students would read 1,000 books in grades 1–12, which is what my numbers more or less add up to. Imagine all our high school graduates having this under their belts. The goal also includes the proviso that this reading has been done pretty much on the students' own volition (with teacher support and guidance), not by forcing them to read specific books or rewarding them with pizza. We'd still have class books and teaching about books, but most of the books would be the students' own choice. A pipe dream? It could happen. Even if not fully, for every student, we could get a lot closer than we are now.[4]

I want to make it really, really clear that a thousand books, or equivalent goals for each year of school, should never become an explicit expectation for students. The focus is on the reading itself, getting engaged with books you enjoy and having the time, in school, to do so. The idea of thirty-five books this year, a thousand books by the end of high school, can be the teacher's secret dream for her students. A goal or slogan to share with students might be "seize the time." They'll never again have so much time for reading. If their time spent reading in school engages them, they'll choose on their own to seize the weekends, seize time under their bedcovers with a flashlight or a tablet reader, and seize the summer for even more reading. They can then finish high school ready to hit the ground running for literacy in their adult lives.

---

[4] Jane Bean-Folkes (personal communication, 2012), a longtime staff developer for the Columbia Teachers College Reading and Writing Project, suggests that my estimates across all grades are, if anything, on the low side, and could perhaps be doubled.

CHAPTER 3

How Hard Should the Books Be, and Why?

Everybody loves books for babies: *Pat the Bunny*, *Goodnight Moon*. But first-graders would be unlikely to be caught reading them other than for nostalgia. Adults would rarely read *Dear Mr. Henshaw*, let alone a *Junie B. Jones* book, for their own recreational reading. Our reading interests mature just as our reading ability does. However, the complexity of what many Americans read may be stalling out at too low a level. Older Americans typically grew up with high school English classes where they were assigned (and *maybe* read) difficult classic books from English and American literature: *Silas Marner*, *The Scarlet Letter*, and so on. Authors were typically white, male, and dead, with the token presence of Jane Austen and Emily Dickinson. This clearly wasn't working. The books weren't just hard, they were boring, and their goal of exposing teenagers to the "great works" of the English language was seen as increasingly less important as a curriculum goal. Very few adults pick up those kinds of books for their personal reading unless they were English majors in college. The goal of a canon didn't go away, but the books got easier. Sandra Stotsky recently (2012) pulled together information from a variety of studies, including one that she conducted in Arkansas, that suggests that American high school students aren't reading very challenging books in English class or on their own. Surveys of teachers show that books read in common in English classes just aren't very hard. (They also aren't very fresh or even very good: the twentieth-century titles most commonly taught feature what I consider middlebrow books of a half-century ago, like *To Kill a Mockingbird*, *Of Mice and Men*, and *Lord of the Flies*.[1])

These changes have come about because of a sense that the goals of an English language arts program can be met through students' reading literature that's interesting, accessible, and meaningful for them, while not abandoning the idea of some kind of canon of good literature. In particular, a lot of the older classics were just too difficult for kids to read, in part because of historical language change. The Common Core State Standards do have a point with their attention to the importance of text complexity. In my view, and I think theirs, high school graduates should be able to read serious adult fiction and nonfiction books; newspapers and current affairs magazines; texts found in a variety of workplaces; and, at some level, medical, financial, and legal materials they encounter in adult life. This is important for all areas of life. First, college courses require sophisticated reading of complex texts: science, mathematics, and business textbooks, not just literature but literary criticism, original sources and analysis in the social sciences, and so on. Second, life as a consumer and citizen increasingly requires the ability to read critically when one sees sales pitches disguised as information, news coverage and commentary with varying degrees of bias, public debate about critical social issues, and other reading that's part of adult life in the world. Third, our personal lives are enhanced by reading literature and nonfiction, and we owe our high school graduates the opportunity to develop their reading ability to the point where they're able to read works that stretch their intellects and emotions. A high school graduate who hasn't read a book more challenging than *To Kill a Mockingbird* is in some ways in no better shape than a fifth-grader who's stuck at the *Frog and Toad* level. Workplace literacy is addressed less directly by the English language arts curriculum, since the reading demands of work tend to be either learned on the job — as in retail sales or office work — or through the worker's training or academic preparation (police work or

---

[1] Readers may disagree with my assessment of these, but they're just not of the quality that is taken seriously in college classes or literary scholarship.

nursing), but they certainly require readers to be able to navigate informational text — perhaps unlike any they've seen previously — effectively and independently.

Many students younger than high school are likely to already be reading text that's complex enough, since they choose their reading based on the maturity of the content. However, they may not be reading enough of it to keep improving, and many of them may begin finding that they're unable to read the books they'd like to, when the subject matter is appropriate but the text itself beyond their reach. Young adult books, a huge genre, continue to appeal to even adult readers, so that high school students may not have a strong impetus to make the stretch into fully adult books.

So How Hard Should the Books Be?

The Common Core State Standards, in their listing of text complexity ("Read and comprehend complex literary and informational texts independently and proficiently") as one of ten standards for every grade level, has foregrounded the issue. Indeed, this expectation is one major way these standards differ from previous ones. However, its goal that students be able to read "grade-level appropriate"[2] material by the end of the academic year is problematic because it focuses on the endpoint, not the process. If you want to pilot a 747, you need to start out on small planes. Here's a better goal, that works for all students: by the end of the school year, be able to read harder books than you were able to at the beginning of the school year. Because of Common Core State Standards expectations, teachers should also have a sense of what the "grade-level" texts for their year look like and monitor students' reading accordingly. But the kids have to start where they are. Reading harder books can best be framed to students as reading more mature books as the year goes on. The larger goal, for grades 1–12, is for all students to

---

[2] This term in itself raises problems, which I'll discuss below.

eventually be prepared for college-level reading, or as close to it as possible, through having read books that are hard enough. We need goals that are reachable, and that students can own; I'll return to the complexity demands of the Common Core State Standards at the end of this chapter.

What Do More Complex Texts Look Like?

If we look at books that students in grades 1–12 may be reading, changes in their complexity are obvious. What I'd like to do here is to establish a way of talking broadly about levels of difficulty and complexity, first with fiction, then nonfiction.

Let's take six well-known and widely read novels as examples of complexity progression. I've included their Accelerated Reader grade levels: *A Kiss for Little Bear* (32 pp., 1.4); *Judy Moody* (176 pp., 3.3); *The Higher Power of Lucky* (160 pp., 5.9); *The Outsiders* (192 pp., 4.7); *The Great Gatsby* (180 pp., 7.3); and *Invisible Man* (581 pp., 7.2). We can refer to them as typifying six roughly categorized levels of reading: early readers, lower elementary grades, upper elementary grades, young adult, adult, and challenging adult.

At this point I'm avoiding the use of any readability formulas; the focus is on helping you to develop a rough sense of the kind of *progression in complexity* that you'd like students to achieve. We're looking here not for the perfectly curated book for whole-class teaching at a particular grade level but for the development of each student's increasingly complex reading throughout a whole school year.

If you took a page from every book a student read from first grade through twelfth and laid them out in a row,[3] you'd see their text complexity gradually increase over the years. Ideally, the progression would be metaphorically like a ramp rather than stair steps, let alone leaps. What constitutes complexity? For our purposes, we can think about three components. First, the sentences get longer and more

---

[3] A thousand pages laid side by side would measure about 500 feet, or a long city block.

complicated; that is, syntactic complexity increases. Here's a typical sentence from each book:

> *Little Bear*: "Everyone came."
>
> *Judy Moody*: "Dad says we have more Band-Aids in our bathroom than the Red Cross."
>
> *The Higher Power of Lucky*: "Lucky had clutched the urn to her chest and stared at the burros and tried to know what to do."
>
> *The Outsiders*: "Soda was awake by then, and although he looked stony-faced, as if he hadn't heard a word the doctor had said, his eyes were bleak and stunned."
>
> *The Great Gatsby*: "And so with the sunshine and the great bursts of leaves growing on the trees, just as things grow in fast movies, I had that familiar conviction that life was beginning over again with the summer."
>
> *Invisible Man*: "Upon hearing that one of the unemployed brothers was an ex-drill master from Wichita, Kansas, I organized a drill team of six-footers whose duty it was to march through the streets striking up sparks with their hob-nailed shoes."

(For those who still remember how to diagram sentences, you could imagine how doing so would illuminate these sentences' increasing grammatical complexity.)

Second, vocabulary gets more difficult. Here are some examples of the more challenging words (for their age level) from each of the six books.

> *A Kiss for Little Bear*: skunks, chat, pond
>
> *Judy Moody*: slimy, pickle, flytrap
>
> *The Higher Power of Lucky*: galaxies, crevices, sweet-smellingness
>
> *The Outsiders*: automatically, perspiration, scatterbrained
>
> *The Great Gatsby*: denizen, monopolizing, roadster
>
> *Invisible Man*: ectoplasms, epidermis, bilious

Books vary widely in the words they use, of course; these words aren't meant to be precisely representative of different vocabulary levels but merely to give some examples of how, as books get harder, rarer words begin to appear. This can be called lexical complexity.

Third, the stories and themes of books vary in complexity. In these six books, in order of complexity, kisses get traded back and forth between animals; a third grader has ups and downs in school; a ten-year-old explores life in her small community and learns to trust her stepmother; a teenager deals with family and gang issues; a man narrates events in the life of his mysterious millionaire neighbor; and a man explores issues of personal and racial identity in a volatile political context. Those who have read all six books will realize that these brief plot summaries only give the smallest hint of how the books differ from each other in content and how that content is explored; simple plots and themes give way to elaborate ones. The first four are age-appropriate for four levels of younger audiences, and while the last two are both adult books, classic ones that would fall on anyone's list of great American novels, *Invisible Man* is appreciably more challenging.

Similarly, I found six informational books on the topic of food at comparable grade levels to contrast; you can get a sense of each of them from using the "Look Inside the Book" feature on Amazon, especially useful for the heavily illustrated first three. *Who Eats What?* (Lauber and Kelly, 1994) has large illustrations with a couple of sentences per page. *How Did That Get in My Lunchbox* (Butterworth, 2005) is also heavily illustrated, but with multiple paragraphs of text on many pages. *Food* (Buller, 2005) follows the Eyewitness Series' usual format of paragraph-sized snippets of interesting information and lively photographs arranged topically by page. *The Omnivore's Dilemma for Kids* (Pollan, 2009) is a young-adult rewriting of the author's best-selling book. For adults, *The American Way of Eating* (McMillan, 2012) is a journalist's extensive recounting of her time spent undercover as a farm laborer, at Walmart, and at Applebee's. *Fear of Food* (Levenstein, 2012) is much more academic, but still suitable for a high school student. Looking at nonfiction books on a similar topic for different ages makes it very clear that complexity also can include the role of background knowledge, nontext features, more technical vocabulary, and depth of information provided. Harder informational books assume more of the reader. (Looking at and talking about books of varied difficulty on the same topic can also be useful to do with students as part of helping them match themselves with the right book.)

How Important Is It to Have the Right Text Complexity Formula?

For the classroom teacher, the issue of which text complexity format to use is virtually irrelevant. There are many readability formulas; the Wikipedia entry on "Readability" gives a good overview with details about specific versions. There's always a tension between a formula's ease of use and its meaningfulness. Formulas based on word length as an indicator of semantic complexity (vocabulary) and sentence length as a measure of syntactic complexity (grammar) are now completely computerized (including on MS Word) but are very crude measures. The more complex methods discussed extensively in Appendix A of the Common Core State Standards are much harder to apply and not at all transparent or usable by a classroom teacher or reader. The most commonly used measures in educational settings are Lexile measures; the ATOS formula used by Accelerated Reader (both of them using sentence length and word frequency/difficulty); and Fountas & Pinnell Leveled Book levels (for books roughly through eighth grade), which take more factors into account. You can easily find levels for most books online, as well as many reading level comparison charts, although the latter aren't always very precise.

But the formulas provide very little guidance in suggesting what students can or should read. Once students have a sense of what's comfortable for them as readers, then readability formulas can be one tool—but a very weak one—for getting a sense of what other books might also be comfortable for or a bit of a stretch for them. (The Fountas & Pinnell levels, however, are appropriate for children to use themselves to choose books.) A far better tool than dependence on formulas, however, is to get children thinking about the appropriate levels within the six ranges of books I mentioned above, from early reader through difficult adult, to think about which books to choose from.[4] At the right time, teachers can talk about the transition from beginning chapter books to longer ones, from books with many to some to no illustrations, from young adult to adult books. These are of course gradual rather than abrupt transitions, with young readers, like adults, not limiting themselves to a single range of books. Within these general ranges, personal interest, length of the book, subject matter, and many other individual choices are far more important than a precise level.

Reading levels can have some (limited) use in practice, but should always be considered optional. Here's what I'd suggest. For students in the elementary grades, the Fountas & Pinnell levels can be useful since they take into account more information than the numerical formulas, and since students' growth from one level to another can be rapid. As described in Chapter 4, they can also be one tool for organizing a classroom library, and they're also simple enough for students to be able to connect to, without the stigma of having a grade-level equivalent attached. They then become a guide for the student for what books to browse in, and where to go when they're ready for a bit more of a challenge. They should *never* be used to limit a student's reading, either to keep them away from reading easier books or prevent them from trying a harder one. (In my experience, English language learners are sometimes prevented from reading books that would be comfortable for them because a running-record assessment has placed them at too low a level, due to first-language influences on pronunciation that are counted as errors.)

I was about to write a paragraph on how Lexile levels can perhaps be useful to get a rough estimate of how hard one book might be compared to another, but then did

---

[4] Picture books are a special case, since their intended audience may be children who are too young to read the book independently, or older than the picture book format would suggest; think of them as their own genre, sometimes more suitable for read-alouds or class books than as the prime source of children's independent reading material. Every classroom that contains picture books should include discussions of how they fit into students' independent reading.

five minutes of research and changed my mind. Here are the six novels I suggested as examples of books appropriate for each of six grade ranges, with their Lexile levels and the grade-level range for the Common Core State Standards that this Lexile level places them in. I've included the grade-level placement both from the original Lexile bands (lexile.com) and from the more rigorous placements found in the Common Core State Standards (Appendix A, p. 8).

Book	Lexile score	Original Lexile grade level	Common Core State Standards grade level
A Kiss for Little Bear	100	1	1
Judy Moody	530	2–3	2–3
The Higher Power of Lucky	1010	9–10	6–8
The Outsiders	750	4–5	2–3
The Great Gatsby	1070	9–10	6–8
Invisible Man	950	6–8	4–5

The only ones whose Lexile grade-level range fit their best appropriate grade level for readers were the two easiest. *The Outsiders* was placed at mid-elementary school level and *Invisible Man* upper elementary. I confess I was a little stunned by this. I knew that these word-length, sentence-length formulas weren't very accurate, but these aren't even in the ballpark. Teachers' judgments of appropriate grade placement for a book (using only my six roughly defined levels) will be more accurate than the lexiles. The illusion of precision of the latter, appearing to make fine distinctions by giving *The Higher Power of Lucky* a Lexile number of 1010 and *Invisible Man* 950, not only doesn't provide the levels of distinction that the three- and four-digit numbers suggest.[5] The levels don't even put these six books in the right order in

---

[5] Actually, they're really two- and three-digit numbers in disguise; since all the Lexile levels are multiples of ten, you won't find a 973, for instance.

relationship to each other. I also checked Accelerated Reader grade levels for these books, which were a little closer to the mark but not good enough, and also not very closely correlated to the Lexile levels. These formulas just aren't valid enough for classroom use.

What Should Our Text Complexity Goals Be for Students?

The Common Core State Standards have made the question of complexity goals an urgent one that we need to take seriously. My answer is, appropriately, complex. How can we know what the standards are expecting students to read, since they don't provide a transparent rating method? Their exemplar texts are just *examples* of difficulty levels and explicitly not the *exemplary* texts that all students should be required to read; and Lexile levels, which are provided for each grade, are unreliable.

The first point of entry is to develop our own sense of how to compare books and think about their appropriateness for different grade levels. We don't need precise numbers for every possible book, but can rely on our own experiences of children and books, reviews, and publishers' suggested grade levels, as well as Fountas/Pinnell levels through eighth grade. Libraries and the Web are also loaded with book lists; I'd especially recommend those at the website of Nancie Atwell's school at Maine, c-t-l. org, where the books are chosen by students (through high school) and the lists updated regularly.

For high school, it's pretty easy to distinguish young adult books (identifiable by how they're marketed) and complexity variations in adult books. In fiction, ideally every student should be able, by the end of high school, to read recent major novels like *Beloved*, *American Pastoral*, and *White Teeth*, as well as somewhat easier books like *The Namesake* and *The Hours*. Think Pulitzer Prizes, National Book Awards, and so on. Complex books can also include nonfiction independent reading, with content-area teachers suggesting readings. The content demands of the high school curriculum in all subjects can make it hard to keep independent reading going, but the English language arts teacher can strongly promote the reasons why it would serve students' own interests to keep up their independent reading and gradually move into more challenging books. Independent reading is the only realistic way to get all kids working up to reading the kinds of books that can continue to enrich their lives—academic, professional, and personal—as adults. Next, we need to think about text complexity for each student: where she is (defined loosely) and what her next steps might be. Students ideally will read books of varying complexity over a school year rather than following a strictly linear progression. The teacher's role, as described in later chapters, is to help all students get settled in books that are just right for them and stretch their reading muscles as the year goes on.

Third, we can think about class books as a way of feeling confident that we've helped even weaker readers grapple with books with more challenging structure and ideas. If you're unsure about, for instance, what an appropriately complex book for fourth grade might be, you could take a look at the exemplar texts in Appendix B of the Common Core State Standards, but with a big, big grain of salt since so many of them are dated and unappealing. However, if you were to choose, for instance, *Bud, Not Buddy* (Curtis, 1999) as a book to explore with the whole class (with appropriate support for students unable to read it on their own), you could feel comfortable that you were working in harmony with the standards.

I'd also recommend thinking about a capstone book for the school year, a book that would be a bit challenging for your students in September but just right for most of them by May, especially in third grade and above when they're able to read longer books that you can spend some time on. An obvious example would be the winner of the Newbery Medal or another major juvenile book award for elementary school. A capstone book for the last months of high school could be a nice culmination of twelve years of reading, with an English department working toward every student's being able to read and discuss it. My picks? *Train Dreams*, by Denis Johnson, or *Home*, by Toni Morrison, both recent, brief but profound, fictional meditations on twentieth-century American history as experienced by everyday people. Read them and see what you think.

Even So, How Do We Know If We're Meeting the Common Core State Standards for Text Complexity?

So how do we know if we're meeting the Standards? This is a difficult question, in part because both the Standards themselves and early elements of their implementation have carried mixed and sometimes confusing messages. The Standards set target Lexile levels for each grade level, and describe at length the kinds of qualitative measures of complexity that are needed for greater accuracy than quantitative measures like lexiles. They also provide annotations of their analysis of the complexity of a few texts, and list multiple texts of different genres that meet their standard for that grade, with the disclaimer that these aren't meant to be required texts but merely examples of complexity. (However, I've heard anecdotally that at least two state departments of education are buying class sets of all the exemplar texts.)

In practice, students will be expected to understand complex texts and demonstrate this ability on the new tests that are being developed for the Standards. I'd like to share an example of how all of this is being played out. I had an exchange on NCTE's Connected Community with an educator from the Kansas about the Newbery Medal winner *Moon over Manifest*. He described how a committee of teachers and librarians had taken seriously the mandate of the Common Core State Standards to explore text complexity thoughtfully rather than formulaically, and decided that the book (set in Kansas) would be a good choice for grades 6–10. (I had earlier commented that since the publisher had recommended the book for ages 9 and up, it felt like an upper-elementary book to me, and that it might be too easy and indeed babyish for high school students.) A year or so after this exchange, PARCC, one of the two consortia developing tests for the Common Core State Standards, released sample test items for reading. One of the tenth-grade ones was to compare a century-old translation of Ovid with a twentieth-century poem by Anne Sexton on the same topic.[6] My point here is that a state put a good deal of effort into taking the goal of text complexity seriously, but that their plans would leave students seriously unprepared for the level of what the Standards are actually expecting students to read. (By the way, *Moon over Manifest*'s Lexile score puts it at the 4–5 grade level, but reading *The Winter Room* by Gary Paulsen with a grade 9–10 Lexile level wouldn't be of much more help to students asked to analyze Ovid and Sexton.)

What exactly is going on here? The Standards explicitly disavow the idea that students should be asked to read the texts that appear as exemplars of complexity levels in Appendix B. Indeed, this is a good thing because the texts in question are an odd grab-bag, including (depending on the grade-level range) old chestnuts, little-read older award winners, books from twenty years ago of no particular quality, far-from-recent translations of world literature, some random technical documents, and so on, along with some good choices, including a few representing current American cultural diversity. But they'd never be chosen by a teacher as the best collection of readings for a particular grade.

At any rate, however, the Standards don't require that a particular set of texts be read. But it's also not really transparent what kids should be reading to meet the text complexity standard, given all the problems with measuring it. Also, a strong focus on teacher-driven exploration of specific, small numbers of complex texts as defined for each grade level could overshadow the importance of students' reading in large volume. And students whose reading ability is nowhere near the point of reading the levels expected for their grade will get little to no value from such teaching. Readers improve most by reading books, the more the better, that are at a level easy enough for them to read on their own, and then, with natural growth and scaffolding from

---

[6] Here's the task: "Use what you have learned from reading 'Daedalus and Icarus' by Ovid and 'To a Friend Whose Work Has Come to Triumph' by Anne Sexton to write an essay that provides an analysis of how Sexton transforms Daedalus and Icarus." Here's a sentence from the Ovid: "He fashioned quills/and feathers in due order-deftly formed/from small to large, as any rustic pipe/prom straws unequal slants."

the teacher, take on *gradually* harder material. A major premise of this book is that students should increase their reading ability and sophistication over time, and it can't be force-fed. I'm sorry, but a struggling fifth-grade reader will not be able to read *The Secret Garden*, written over 100 years ago and full of British regional dialect, no matter how many lessons a teacher does on it. A focus on text complexity shouldn't *take the place of* extensive independent reading; in fact, the latter is the major *avenue* for achieving the ability to read complex text, with appropriate teaching as I describe in Chapters 9 and 10.

Therefore, perhaps the best choice for teachers who are concerned about meeting the complexity standard is to proceed as I've described in this chapter, by helping students move at an appropriate pace into somewhat harder books over the course of the year. To protect yourself in the face of mandates, I'd include a few of the better examples from each category for each grade-level range of the exemplar texts to include in the classroom library and perhaps use for class books.

PART TWO

How to Do It

4

Get the Books

Kids can't become readers without books. I'm not saying that people read only books, and we certainly should encourage reading in any format, especially for reluctant readers, but I believe that books should be our primary focus in the reading curriculum. Kids will manage to find magazines, comic books, and websites (and it's of course great to have all of these in the classroom), but they could miss out on exposure to adequate numbers of books if we don't make it happen.

Also, kids cannot become strong readers by reading only the amount of text in a basal reader program. Nor is it enough to read only four books a year in their entirety (along with twenty to thirty-seven shorter texts) in fifth grade, for instance, as suggested by the PARCC Model Content Frameworks provided for the Common Core State Standards (www.parcconline.org/sites/parcc/files/PARCCMCFforELALiteracyGRADE5_FINAL_Aug2012_0.pdf). Children of poverty can't become strong readers if they don't have access to *enough* books, as they often don't (McQuillan, 1998). If children are going to read up to a thousand books from grades 1 to 12, they'll need access to perhaps five thousand books over those years to have enough to choose from. This can't be stressed enough. Library funding has become more precarious over the years, largely because of declining local tax revenues. Far too many libraries in small communities have closed, and urban ones have cut back their hours.

Yet books in many forms are more plentiful than ever. In 1950, the population of the United States was half of what it is now, 150 million as compared to over 300 million. Yet in 1950, there were only 11,450 books published in the United States registered for copyright[1] (*Catalog of Copyright Entries*, 1950, retrieved from Google-Books), whereas in 2010, 328,259 new books and editions were published (http://en.wikipedia.org/wiki/Books_published_per_country_per_year). That is, book publishing has grown fourteen times as much as population. Children's publishing has not just blossomed, it's exploded, and the books are better and more varied. This is because of a bigger American population and decreased costs of printing, including color printing and other innovations like pop-up books.

So what books should we get for kids, how many, and how? Let's focus primarily on the classroom library, since this will be students' primary source of books, particularly in elementary school and especially for children of poverty with few other literacy resources. A good school library is also important, but you need a lot of books in the classroom itself.

Fountas and Pinnell (2006) provide detailed specifications for classroom libraries for independent reading at different grade levels, around 300 titles in grades 1–8 (plus collections of multiple copies of fifty to ninety-nine titles for guided reading). The lists are broken down by reading level. Richard Allington (2012) suggests that there be at least 500 books in a classroom library, or preferably 1,500. What I provide here are criteria and dimensions of what the classroom library should look like.

---

[1] This is the only statistic I could find indicative of the number of books published.

1. Your book collection needs to accommodate the range of readers in your classroom.

You need to have books easy enough for the weakest readers in your classroom and challenging enough for the strongest ones, and you may need to add books at new levels as you get to know who your students are. Fountas and Pinnell (2006) describe what this should look like for typical classrooms in grades 1–8: about ten levels per grade. Your first-week-of-school conferences with students will show you if you need to expand the range of levels you already have. For a classroom library for high school students, think particularly about finding some appealing books for less proficient and reluctant readers, since they'll need more guidance in finding books than the stronger readers will. It's also important that the books for the weaker readers not seem babyish. Nonfiction books written for slightly younger audiences often work. For instance, young adult informational books will still be appropriate in high school, and upper elementary ones in middle school. Even for adults, a nonfiction book written for young readers is a good way of learning more about a topic on which you'd never read a 500-page adult book. (The history of salt, anyone? Mark Kurlansky wrote a 500-page adult book about it in 2003, followed by a heavily illustrated forty-eight-page children's version in 2006, which is actually pretty engaging.)

You also should do your best to find appropriate first-language books for English language learners who aren't yet proficient in English and ideally for those who are as well. Public libraries have done very well in providing books to suit the languages of their communities, which you can borrow yourself or steer students to. There are also newspapers in other languages available in big-city newsstands and online.

2. Your collection needs a mix of literary and popular books.

It's not about deciding between Newbery Medal winners and series books, it's about having both. Series and other lighter books, many of which catch fire among communities of children, are great sparks to voracious, can't-put-it-down reading. Back in the day it was the Bobbsey Twins, a few decades ago it was Goosebumps, today it's Captain Underpants and the Hunger Games and Wimpy Kid, tomorrow who knows what? Serious adult readers often gulped down entire "subliterary" series as children (Ross, 1995). These books build speed and stamina and keep kids engaged. Publishers also have a lot of nonfiction series; a fun one is *You Wouldn't Want to [Be a Samurai]!* and so on, exploring various grisly eras in history.

We can talk roughly about two categories of books, everyday books and prize contenders. The first group, typically in paperback, are often series commissioned by publishers who develop them and assign writers to them. The illustrations are adequate but not usually by well-known illustrators. The second group are developed by the writer and at least have aspirations of being eligible for awards. They're usually published first in hardcover, sometimes with a paperback following in a year or so if sales warrant it. In nonfiction, the second group are often written by experts in the field, sometimes with a co-author who has written for children before, and containing high-quality illustrations, typically original art or photography, not stock photos. These better books are the ones you'll want to use for class teaching since there's more to say and understand about them, but they also become increasingly important for independent reading, to ramp up students' vocabulary, ability to read complex text, and literary and informational smarts.

We'd like to hear students making comments like, "I read all the Junie B. Jones books a couple of years ago, but now I like books that make me think and learn, not just laugh. I also like reading to learn about the world." We need to provide the range of books that help them start where they are but keep expanding and moving on up. They may also move to more mature series books as they move through the grades:

think *Sweet Valley Twins* to *Sweet Valley High* to *Twilight* to *Game of Thrones* to Jane Austen's books.[2]

3. Your collection needs to be varied in topic, genre, length, format, whatever.

You should look for a roughly 50/50 mix of fiction and nonfiction. Then within each of those groupings you should have a mix of maybe 60 percent everyday and series books, 40 percent higher quality. (All of these percentages are very rough; see what works for you and your students.) Young children's books used to be primarily stories, but there's now nonfiction for all ages. In high school, subject-area classes should have, if not classroom libraries, at least annotated bibliographies of relevant subject-area nonfiction, including both young adult books and those written for general adult readers.

There are many, many sources for recommended book titles. I'm going to mention some major ones here, and a librarian can suggest others. (Your public library is also likely to have some of the book-length guides on their reference shelves.) If you're building a classroom library from scratch, you can use a resource like *The Horn Book Guide Online* (www.hornbookguide.com/cgi-bin/hbonline.pl); short-term subscriptions and a free demo are available. A good college children's literature textbook will also have extensive booklists and provide you with a comprehensive view of the literature involved. Two that I like are Lynch-Brown, Tomlinson, and Short, 2011 for children's books, and Tomlinson and Lynch-Brown, 2010 for young adult. They're expensive, but there are earlier editions of them, often just a few years old, available for bargain prices online. I'd really recommend getting one of these books for your reference library; they also mention many connections to Internet resources. If you need to assemble a classroom library quickly, the *Field Guide to the Classroom Library* series from

---

[2] Okay, not quite a series, but I couldn't resist.

Teachers College, though a little dated, lists and annotates a full classroom collection for each grade level.

Be sure to include adequate numbers of books by and about people of color, since they're still underrepresented in books published and therefore in lists of recommended books (Ehrlich, 2011). The website www.multiculturalchildrenslit.com/ links to a number of other sources, as well as suggesting some specific titles. Jane Gangi also has created a lengthy categorized bibliography of children's books with many multicultural titles (www.wcsu.edu/sps/gangi/gangi-collection-2010.pdf). Such books are important for children of color to see themselves in what they read, but also for white Anglo American students to see books about people who make up the rest of America. Indeed, everyone needs to read about the rest of the world too; see Lehman, Freeman, and Scharer (2010).

For current books, I'll suggest a publication and two websites. Horn Book magazine, published six times a year, is my favorite source of reviews of children's books, which are curated in the sense that the journal reviews a limited number of books (perhaps 100 per issue, 600 a year), all of them worthwhile, and have about a dozen starred books per issue, compiled annually in a Fanfare list (www.hbook.com/2012/12/choosing-books/horn-book-fanfare-1938-to-present/). The titles range from preschool through high school. The other half of each issue is made up of articles on current trends and topics, as well as the acceptance speeches of each year's major award winners. The Horn Book website, although it doesn't contain the full contents of the magazine, has selected articles and, especially important, a variety of book lists (http://archive.hbook.com/resources/books/default.asp). The *New York Times Book Review* also reviews children's books (all ages) regularly; you can find an archive by going to nytimes.com and searching for "children's books," which will take you to a number of interesting links. (Sorting by relevance and limiting the search to the last twelve months will give you a good sampling.)

I've just scratched the surface here of how to find books, as there are many other curated lists from organizations like the National Council of the Social Studies, an especially good one (www.socialstudies.org/notable). Also look at award winners beyond the Newbery and Caldecott, such as the Orbis Pictus award from NCTE for nonfiction (www.ncte.org/awards/orbispictus). But I've provided you with enough resources to either begin or keep updating a classroom library.

4. The books have to be fresh and look good.

Curate your collection. Don't just bring in every book you've saved from your own childhood or random boxes of stuff from garage sales.[3] Always keep the dust jacket on hardcover books, laminating if necessary for preservation. Keep it fresh by adding new books throughout the year; borrow a marketing tool from bookstores by having a "new arrivals" table. You can create the same effect by not having all of your existing library shelved and on display at the beginning of the year, so that the new arrivals can be pulled from storage as well as freshly acquired. If you have some old classics that kids are still reading but are no longer in good physical condition, consider buying cheap replacements online. For instance, used Harry Potter books are available for $4.00, including shipping, on Amazon. Weed your collection, perhaps with the help of students. Older books that no longer interest kids can be moved to a back cupboard (since we all have such a hard time discarding books!) and then moved to the bargain bin when we realize we haven't missed them.

5. The books need to be organized and accessible.

This is complicated, because it can be useful to categorize books in different ways, such as difficulty level and topic. How you organize your books will differ a good deal depending on what grade level you teach. It also doesn't hurt to take a look at how libraries and bookstores organize children's books. Here are some categorization ideas to think about. If possible, involve students in setting up and maintaining the

---

[3] One appropriate place for books you've acquired or have weeded out that aren't good enough to be on the shelves is a bargain bin, like public libraries and thrift stores often have; put them in a crate and invite kids to paw through them and take one home for free.

categories, and rethinking them if necessary. Certainly help your students understand them. The goal of organizing books is twofold: promoting browsing among books of different types, and being able to find a specific book.

Guided reading levels in bins or on shelves

This is a valuable tool (although only one) for helping students move up on their own in the complexity of the books they read, by moving from one shelf or bin to the next. (By high school, of course, it's no longer relevant.) If books don't have a spine, they need to be in bins or the equivalent, so that you can see the covers. Thicker books can go on shelves, and should if possible be organized by at least the first letter of the author's last name. Try taping the level of the book and the letter for the author on the spine, perhaps in different colors, and alphabetize within levels. Leave some room or assign another space to display some of your books cover-forward.

Genres and/or topics

The age of your students, the number of books you have, and the level of sophistication you're working at will help to determine these categories. My current favorite bookstore, McNally Jackson in New York City, subcategorizes its fiction geographically: American, Asian, African, and so on (including Canadian, reflecting the owner's origins). This adds a whole layer of pleasure to browsing. Another New York bookstore, St. Mark's Bookshop in the East Village, has an anarchy section. I'll never buy anything from it, but it has its audience. Know *your* customers, know your kids. Organizing by topic includes simple strategies like subcategorizing if you have more than a single bin of level B books (even if just fiction and nonfiction), or creating a special shelf of books set in Georgia if that's where you live. Students in upper elementary and middle school might like having separate fiction sections for sci-fi and dystopian, kids from other countries, fantasy, adventure, urban, and so on. The best way to find out what categories to use is to notice what kids are reading and talk to them, which ends up being a teaching opportunity.

A goal for a lesson on subcategorizing fiction would be for students to understand that many authors write books that follow the conventions of a genre or category, which may or may not have a name. Invite students to mention fiction that they've read recently, and see if there are obvious groupings within the books that they name. One big grouping will be "realistic stories about American kids today," but within that group, some are more about girls, some more about boys, some in cities, some in suburbs, some white kids, some Latino kids, kids of different ages, kids from different states, kids with pets, kids with family problems. Talking about these different topics and focuses may not result in shelving all the books according to such categories, but it'll get students thinking about the range of what's there, and could provide ideas for tags in an online database of your classroom library, which I'll talk about below. Classroom libraries are less common in high school, but a classroom with a library of American fiction, for instance, perhaps in connection with the Common Core State Standards, might find it useful to have it shelved according to century or other relevant categories.

The Dewey Decimal System

When I suggest using the Dewey Decimal System to teachers, they show no interest, and tend to know little about it themselves. However, I think it's tremendously valuable for students to learn about, probably beginning in upper elementary grades, since it's the system likely to be used in public libraries, for both children's and adult books, for the foreseeable future. We usually think of the DDS as a search and retrieval tool (look up the book's number and find it on the shelf), not a conceptual one, but it's an organized system for categorizing knowledge that can make you a savvier user of the library.

A kids' guide to the Dewey Decimal System appears as the Appendix. Here's how I'd use it to open a discussion about how to organize or navigate the classroom library. "In 1876, a guy named Melvil Dewey set up a way to put any book in a numbered category so that books in a library on related topics would be near each other on the shelves. There are a lot of things that books can be about, so he had a lot of categories. The great part is that there are categories within categories, so that you can look at smaller groups of ideas within one topic. Here's an example . . .

To write on the board as you proceed:

500: Science

590: Animals

599: Mammals

599.3: Mammals of the ocean

599.35: Dolphins

All books about basic science are in the 500s. Books about animals are in the 590s. Books about mammals are numbered 599. Since there are different kinds of mammals, Dewey went into decimal points after the 599. Books about ocean mammals are 599.5, and dolphins, a kind of ocean mammal, are 599.53. What do you think about setting up our classroom nonfiction library using this system? You can look up any book's Dewey Decimal number online, so it'll be easy to label the books. Dewey thought of everything. Call number 999 is for books about life on other planets. Really!"

I've mentioned it here in relation to the classroom library, but learning about the Dewey Decimal System helps create smarter, more resourceful readers. Just looking at the system of categories (my version is modified from the official one—not the numbers, just which headings I included—to be child-friendly) can get students thinking about what topics they might want to learn more about, and connect them directly to a browsing trip at the school or public library.

6. You need shelves to put the books on.

Before long, children's reading may be primarily on devices, but for now we need physical space for them. In planning for this, think of a good bookstore children's section as a model for arrangement. A teacher education student of mine told me that in a classroom where he was observing, the books that children were most likely to be interested in reading were on shelves not only too high for them to reach but too high for even an adult to read the titles. Classrooms vary widely in what kinds of shelving they have, so you may have to improvise. Remember, not all books need to be on display at all times. You might have the most popular books always on shelves and others as a rotating collection, depending on your energy for moving books around.

7. Catalog (keep a record of) your books.

Several years ago, I would have thought this would be too much work, but online resources have made it doable. I've been using librarything.com for years now. Here's how it works. Go to the site and create an account. All they ask is a username and password, so there are no privacy issues. It's free for up to 200 books; after that there's a lifetime fee of $25. (You could avoid the fee by starting a second account; for instance, from the beginning you could set up separate usernames for your fiction and nonfiction collections.) Then you click on "Add books" and start finding your books. All you have to do is enter about as much information as you would to find a book on Amazon (e.g., "spinelli maniac") and it'll give you a list of titles to choose from. You add your book, then when you click on "View books" you'll see them all displayed. Then you can sort and re-sort your collection by author, title, or whatever you want. The process is easy enough for kids to help with entering the data.

To see all the features it has, go to and see the sample collection I've set up at librarything.com/collection/qandq, with a couple of different display styles that include different information. The tag and comment columns can be used to indicate where you've shelved the books or any other information you want, and your students can access the list from any computer. Lexile levels and Dewey Decimal numbers are available for many books automatically.

So how do you pay for all these books for your classroom library? Some schools and communities have more resources than others.[4] If money is an issue for you with building a classroom library, here are some ideas. Within your school, see if less money can be spent on textbooks and other commercial materials, which are often very high-priced. Talk to the PTA; if you're in a high-poverty school, see if your PTA can partner with one from a richer school. Use your school and public libraries to rotate groups of books in and out of your classroom library. Explore websites where donors are invited to contribute to individual teachers and their classrooms, such as donorschoose.org. (If exploring this option, the more specific the request the better: for instance, "Help me buy this list of fifty paperback novels set in each of the fifty states so that my students can learn more about their country.")

Finally, perhaps part of being a teacher is spending some of your own money; if you do so already, you can focus that spending on books; skip buying stickers and other paraphernalia. There are a lot of copies of titles from popular book series floating around, on Amazon and — if you have the time — at yard sales and thrift stores. Higher-quality books will come out in paperback or turn up used on Amazon after they've been out for a while. Teachers have sometimes had luck going on eBay and searching for, for instance, "fifth-grade books" and finding collections of books that add up to less than a dollar per title, often from retiring teachers.

---

4. This is a larger issue, for which larger, political solutions would be best. In New York City, two consecutive mayors, Giuliani and Bloomberg, have provided funding for libraries for every classroom, including replacement funds to allow for attrition. Since we're now going to have new standards at the state level, wouldn't governors' classroom libraries be a good idea? Or Presidents', for that matter?

Of course, people working for big corporations don't have to scout on eBay for the tools they need to do their jobs. Schools are traditionally underfunded, so buying books for kids with your own money may just have to go with the territory of being a teacher (there's a tax deduction, too); try thinking about building a curated classroom library over the course of your career. With careful planning, including sources of good new books every year[5] and maybe special topics that are unique to your classroom (my kids are going to rock dinosaurs!), you can build a classroom library to be proud of.

---

[5] Try looking at booklists from the year before, from which many titles will have dropped in price or be available used on sites such as Amazon.com.

5

Set Up the Program

L et's get to it then. This chapter is where I provide the framework of the "read more books, read harder books" model. It incorporates elements of, and owes a debt to, ideas that have been around for decades, but sets a new goal in service of a new vision. First, read more. Think about how much time you can get kids to spend actually reading. More on this later, but given its importance, it should be a priority in the school day, particularly for those who aren't reading outside of school. Second, ramp it up. Always be thinking and talking to students about whether, in some of their reading, they're wondering about whether they're ready to push a little beyond what they're reading now, which is likely to involve trying out more sophisticated books gradually, not for all of their reading.

Once students are proficient enough to read independently (see Chapter 8), we can set up classroom programs based on volume and complexity of reading in which the components mentioned on pages 3–4 are central. Let's talk about what this looks like in a classroom, and then go on in later chapters to look at the books and the teaching and the documentation. The model is basically the same for all grade levels. The model can also work in conjunction with an existing readers' workshop, which it parallels in many ways, or with a mandated program, with some adaptations. In secondary school, it can be used just in English language arts but would ideally involve coordination across all subject areas.

Beginning the School Year

The first week of school is a time to get to know who your students are as readers. The most important information to find out about them is their identities as readers, what their interests are, and a rough sense of their proficiency. During the first few days I'd use a combination of class discussions, questionnaires, and individual conferences to gather this data.

Using Summer Reading to Kick Off the School Year and as a Class Barometer

What we want students to learn and to internalize through the lesson is the idea of "reader's identity," of having reading as a part of their lives. Every day includes physical life (eating, sleeping, exercise), social life (family, friends), and mental life (thinking, talking, media, reading, and so on). Reading may not yet be part of how your students conceptualize their lives, but it will be. It's a big part of what their year with you will be all about. Talking about summer reading will let you know what you have to work with as kids' reading identities. As you read through these teaching ideas, think also about doing a similar lesson at the end of the school year about planning and setting goals for the next summer's reading.

Ideally, you can begin by modeling what you read over the summer, with books in hand to show the students. Perhaps some children's or young adult books that you'll be adding to the classroom library, a professional book that's given you some new ideas for your teaching, a book on cooking, gardening, or another personal interest, and an adult novel or two. Make it real! If summer reading for you is all about chick lit, techno-thrillers, and other beach books, bring those in and talk about them. If you don't read during the summer, talk about that and, ideally, why you wish you did read more or what you hope to do to get back into reading. The point of this modeling is to create a climate where reading is understood as something that we choose to do, have reasons for doing, and crave time for.

Then turn it over to the kids. Pair-share followed by group share is a good way to do it, a strategy that you'll be using with them throughout the year. Recognize that not everyone will have read during the summer, and address this by asking them to share something about what they might have liked to read and what would have made them more likely to do so. They also might have read in formats other than books, such as magazines or screens, which they can be encouraged to mention. During the group discussion, look for opportunities for questions about how they discovered a book, what they did or didn't like about it, and if they'd recommend it to a classmate. You can end the discussion by asking students to reflect on whether thinking about their summer reading has gotten them thinking about reading for the fall.

What if your kids for the most part didn't read during the summer? There are certainly communities where reading isn't a regular part of life. They may be communities of poverty with little access to books, or wealthy communities where adults' and children's lives are heavily scheduled. We all live in twenty-first-century communities where screens have taken over much of what pages used to do. Your school may be a place where the volume of reading among students isn't high (for instance, if scripted curriculums are used, or if students are assigned but don't complete reading). All of this is part of what this first-day summer reading conversation is meant to explore: you're checking the literacy temperature of your classroom community to discover where you're starting. But you're also showing that having a reading life is something you'll be expecting, indeed taking for granted, even if it's been dormant for many of your students.

As a follow-up to this class meeting, ask each student to write as much as they can about their summer reading: what they read, finding books, what it was like for them, whether they would have liked to have read more. You can explain to them that this is a way for you to get to know each one of them as a reader as you start the school year, so that the more information they can give you about their summer reading, the better. You might also use this as the first entry for students in a reader's notebook or reflection journal. It might be fun, if budget allows, to buy some notebooks that are a little bit special; stationery stores and bookstores are full of them. Little binders that pages can be added to are an especially good choice.[1] If you have a classroom of reluctant or struggling readers who didn't read over the summer, invite them to write what a summer that includes pleasure reading could be like, or skip the writing for now. Or you could invite them to write about their top five memories of the summer, and use this to learn more about the interests that they might connect to in books.

As you read the students' writing about their summer reading or conference with them, you might want to draw up a checklist, where for each student you note the following:

Amount read	__ High	__ Low
	__ Medium	__ None
Access to books	__ Good	__ Poor
	__ Some	
Enthusiasm for reading	__ Strong	__ Limited
	__ Okay	__ Negative
Range of reading	__ Varied	__ Narrow
Title of one book read:	Level of book:	

---

[1] I love the Circa notebook systems from Levenger.com, although they're a little expensive for classroom use. You might find them useful for teacher purposes, though.

Assessing Students' Interests and Self-Concepts as Readers

The second task in starting the year is assessing students' interests and self-concepts as readers. There are many questionnaires and forms for assessing reading attitudes; see Serafini (2010) and Rhodes (1993) for examples. What I've provided here is a short version, with only five questions, that you can use in at least three ways: as the focus of a class discussion, for individual conferences with each student, or as a written questionnaire. All modes of doing this are useful, and the one you choose is likely to depend on factors such as class size, age and writing proficiency of your students, and personalities of your students. The goal is twofold: to get students thinking about their reading preferences, and to inform you about starting points. This activity can of course be repeated and modified in all three formats throughout the school year in addition to its use at the beginning of the year as a kickoff. You can also share your own answers to these questions with students as appropriate.

Here are the questions (modify as appropriate for age level or otherwise):

1. Favorites: What's a book that you really liked, whether you read it yourself or someone read it to you? Is there anything other than a book that you read and really liked?

2. Genres: Of these types of books, what ones would you like most and least: stories about kids/people like you; stories about kids/people different from you; stories that couldn't really happen (i.e., fantasy and sci-fi); information about people and places; information about nature and science; information about technology? Any others I haven't mentioned?

3. Range: Do you like reading a lot of different kinds of stuff, or prefer to read things that are similar in some way?

4. Volume: Compared to other kids your age, do you think you read a lot, about average, or less than average? Any comments about this?

5. Interest and identity: Are you a kid who loves to read, likes to read, can take it or leave it, or doesn't really like it? Any comments about this?

Determining Your Students' Proficiency as Readers

Many schools already have an assessment of reading level built into their reading curriculum, often as required documentation. What I'm suggesting here is a relatively simple procedure so that you can get your program up and running. You'll need to have at hand a collection of sample reading material that's likely to reflect the range of your students. The best comprehensive resource available for this is *Leveled Books* (Fountas & Pinnell, 2006), which is also a useful book to have on hand for reference about how to assess book levels and match them with readers. However, there are also many free online resources for book levels available, many of them searchable databases. Fountas and Pinnell also have a low-fee searchable database at Heinemann.com. A Google search for "leveled books" will return multiple results. The Fountas and Pinnell levels, also known as Guided Reading levels, intended for grades K–8, are used on many of these sites. These are somewhat imprecise measures, but the best available and useful to get a general sense of what books might be about right for each reader at the beginning of the school year. They're tools, not determiners. These levels top out at Z, which is considered adult. For high school you're best off using your own judgment for books that go beyond this, since Lexile and other levels aren't very reliable at all. To do this assessment with high school students, I'd pick 4–5 books with age-appropriate content but ranging in difficulty such as *The House on Mango Street*, *Fahrenheit 451*, *The Great Gatsby*, and *Pride and Prejudice*.

Here are the steps involved. First, gather a collection of books representing what feels like an appropriate range for your classroom. One book that would be of interest to your students at each appropriate Guided Reading level is enough to have on hand. (*Leveled Books* suggests a specific benchmark book for each level.) If you have older, limited-proficiency readers, try to find books at easier levels that won't seem babyish; I'd recommend high-interest, easy-reading nonfiction paperbacks found easily in libraries and bookstores. (You might try some books from the *Step into Reading* series, where you can look inside the book online to get a sense of the difficulty of the different levels.) You need only one book per level for this assessment. This mini-collection isn't expensive to assemble, and you'll be able to use it for years. You may, of course, already have appropriate choices in your classroom.

Next, arrange a conference with each student in a location where you can lay out your sample books. The tenor of the conversation should of course be appropriate for the age and grade level of the student. Begin by asking, "How do you know when a book is just right for you, rather than too hard or too easy?" (If the student makes only comments like, "If it's about dogs, it's just right for me," clarify by asking if there are dog books that are harder and easier for them.) In schools that use Guided Reading levels, the student may actually say "I'm a Level M," but even so, you'll want to hear what they have to say in their own words about their own sense of the rightness of a difficulty level of a book: "Have you ever tried a book that was too hard? How did you know it was? What does a book that's too easy feel like?"

Then ask the reader for a title of a book that was just right for her, and pick (or have her pick) a book from your grouping that seems comparable. Ask her to look through it, see if it seems like a reasonable choice, and then pick a passage to read aloud, typically about 100–300 words, depending on the student's level. Tell her you'll be asking her about what she read when she's finished. Don't provide any help if she gets stuck; tell her ahead of time that you'll want her to just do whatever she'd do if you weren't there. Position yourself so that you can see the book over her shoulder as she reads, or you could have photocopies of passages you've selected from each book to read along from and make notations on.

During the reading, you'll want to notice rate and fluency (not words per minute but a sense of flow); how often the reader seems stuck or fumbles, the quality of any miscues made[2] and whether they're corrected, how many words the reader seems not to know or recognize, and a general sense of engagement. Don't try to do detailed counts, just take informal notes. If the book seems obviously too hard, you can interrupt the reading and suggest trying an easier one. When she finishes, say in an open-ended way, "Tell me about what you just read," with follow-up questions or

---

2 Primarily whether they damage the meaning of the text.

probing as indicated. Then comes the most important question: "Tell me how this book felt for you—too hard, too easy, or just right." Your conversation at this point will of course be informed by your own impressions from the reading and retelling. You could say, for instance, "I notice that you seemed not to know this word, but what kind of sense did you get of what it might mean?" or "You stumbled some at first, but then seemed to pick up speed." Based on your own sense and the reader's responses, you can decide whether this book seems about right or whether you should try out another one. At the end of the session, write a brief summary of your conference.

There are, of course, entire books written about reading assessment, but this isn't a technical assessment for institutional purposes, just a rough-and-ready indicator of each student's approximate level of reading proficiency at the beginning of the year. Although you're likely to repeat the procedure throughout the year to inform your instruction, your goal here is just to get enough information to start the student reading. The first day of school should include a chunk of time for self-selected reading, and by the end of the first week, you should have the knowledge that every student has a book she's able to read comfortably.

I talk later about how to help students figure out which books are best for them to choose from, using both leveling information and their own judgment, but I'd like to mention here how these initial conferences will differ across the grades.

Beginning: For beginning readers in the earliest grades, you need to find out which children are able to read independently—that is, pick up and read a book they haven't seen before. At the beginning of first grade, typically some will and some won't. (How to get kids reading independently as quickly as possible is one subject of Chapter 8.) In first and second grade, where growth in reading proficiency is very rapid, arranging books by Guided Reading or other levels is a useful self-selection tool, so that after the conference, you can suggest, for instance, "Why don't you try the books in the bin labeled 'F' and see how they work for you?"

Intermediate: Children in grades 3–5 will be able to have more self-awareness of the idea of text difficulty; if your books are labeled by level (which I'd recommend if it seems useful for students and used just as a neutral tool, not a determiner), you might share your sense of a child's approximate reading level from the conference and suggest exploring books ranging from one level below to one level above that, as well as not being afraid to try any book that looks interesting.

Middle school: At this age, levels may matter less than what books are popular with peers or otherwise of interest, and you can suggest that students think about trying shorter books and then longer ones, and about transitioning from children's to young adult books as they feel both more proficient and ready for more challenging reading.

High school: English language arts is just one subject in the school day, and you'll need a plan for how independent reading fits in with any books required by your school's or district's curriculum. A good conversation after the initial proficiency conference would involve talking about what kinds of reading the student would like to do during the year, or at least right now. Since at this age students are less likely to find their independent reading books in the classroom than in a library, bookstore, or on a device, a starter booklist for the class — twenty to forty books ranged roughly by difficulty level, with annotations — could be a valuable kickstarter, without your needing to have copies of all the books. Content-area teachers could provide similar books.

Scheduling the Classroom Reading Block

Once you have the year up and running, the next step is to think about what each day's reading time will look like in your classroom. This will look often dramatically different across grades 1–12, so I'm going to focus on essential and desirable components of how to spend the time. This isn't an entire primer on how to implement a readers' workshop but a general framework for it. None of it is written in stone, so think about what works for you. These components can then be developed in ways that suit the age and grade level of your students, any curriculum you're already using, and the amount of support your students need with their reading. Other authors have suggested specific daily schedules, and I'd recommend their books for detailed schedules and plans for different grade levels. (See Taberski, 2000, for primary; Serafini, 2001, for upper elementary; and Atwell, 1998, for middle school and secondary.)

Giving Kids Time to Read

This goes back to the original sustained silent reading model from half a century ago. Kids need time in school to read. How much? Enough time to get absorbed in what they're reading. For young children, I'd start with about seven minutes, using a timer, and add a minute a day, discussing with them whether the amount of time feels comfortable and gradually increasing to twenty or thirty minutes. I believe that a good range of time to aim for across all grades is thirty to sixty minutes a day (or longer). If it's too long for kids at first, start shorter and work up. In high school, where a period may be only forty-five minutes long, obviously students can't read that much every day in English language arts class, so you'll need other solutions. Schoolwide solutions are best, such as reading time spread across multiple courses or a daily silent reading time for the whole school. An English language arts teacher working on his own could have silent reading for part of each period or one day a week (see Atwell's discussion, 1998), but also needs to work with students to set goals for time spent reading outside of school, perhaps in lieu of other kinds of homework.

One consideration in determining the length of school time spent reading is whether the students are likely, realistically, to be reading outside of school. For many, school is the only place where the books are. Some thirty years ago, I did a workshop at a school whose teachers resisted the idea of spending class time on reading. Astonishingly, this was despite the school's being in a Native American community where the nearest bookstore was sixty miles away and many of the parents were nonliterate, English language learners, or both. But not reading outside of school is an issue regardless of location and social class. I'd only consider lowering the in-school reading time if I had strong evidence that all students were reading outside of school.

The time set aside for independent reading also needs to be spent actually reading, mostly silently (with accommodations for young children who haven't transitioned to silent reading yet, some partner reading, and so on). Students need to have their books at the ready, including back-ups if they're likely to finish the one they're on. It's not a time for general homework, or browsing the bookshelves. (The teacher can have a small stack for handing a book to a kid who left hers at home.) This expectation of silence and minimal movement in the classroom is crucial to having this really be a reading time.

Comfort helps; sitting at a desk may be the least conducive posture for getting really engaged in a book. When possible, think beanbag chairs, cushions, tents, and so on (although this is harder to do as kids get older and their bodies get bigger, but see what they suggest). All of these logistical arrangements should be accompanied by class discussions and procedural mini-lessons, so that a class develops expectations as a community for how to use the time.

Opinions differ about how the teacher should spend the reading time. Two alternatives make the most sense. First, the teacher reads during reading time. The advantages are maintaining the silent atmosphere; modeling reading as something everyone does; and having the teacher be seen as another member of the community when it comes to sharing and discussing reading. This model is my own preference, and it has a record of success (McCracken and McCracken, 1978). In fact, some schools over the years have had DEAR (Drop Everything and Read) time when everyone, from the principal to the custodians to visitors, reads at the same time every day.

The other legitimate use of the teacher's time during silent reading time, however, is to conduct individual conferences, with the idea that the teacher's time is too valuable to spend just reading when she could be working with individual students. If so, it's important that it be as nondisruptive to the rest of the class as possible, ideally in a far corner of the room. Reading time is *not* a time to sit at your desk doing paperwork; it can give students the message that you're just giving them a study-hall time so you can get your own "work" done. In my view, it's also not a good idea to patrol the room monitoring behavior or even dipping in to chat briefly with the students about their reading, since it's too interruptive.

Encouraging Readers to Share

Having students talk about what they've read is a simple and powerful component of the individual reading program. I begin the first day of my college reading methods classes by asking the students to choose a children's novel from a pile on a table, and then we all read for several minutes. This is followed by a pair-share of about five minutes and a whole-class discussion of what we've read. I take an active role in commenting about the books, making connections across texts, asking for their views about how the book began, and so on. In the first half-hour of my college class, these prospective teachers have experienced a big chunk of what a successful reading program for children should look like.

As we debrief the experience, I unpackage what I did in my teacher role and what we accomplished. First, I read along with them, so I could take part in the sharing as a full member. Second, I walked around during the pair-shares, eavesdropping and chiming in on their conversations. This gave me a sense of how students were responding to the books: both whether they liked them, and how they chose to talk about them. In the large group, I start off by saying, "Who'd like to share something about their book with the whole group?" As several students share, they're learning about more books from each other, and I'm commenting on them in ways that help educate the whole class: "That won the Newbery Medal; do you all know what that is?"; "You knew from the beginning that this book was going to be sad; do you think you'll want to finish it?"; "Jack Gantos is interesting because he's written for all ages from primary to young adult." These comments are off the cuff, based on students' responses to the books, but they're focused on pushing forward their knowledge and thinking.

Doing an informal pair-share and group share every day with kids is extremely powerful. Everybody gets a chance to speak during the pair-share; everyone gets to hear about a lot of books during the group share; the teacher gets a chance to teach responsively, that is, by working in the moment to inform and query students about the books they're reading right then as well as raising other thoughts about literature that may not be a part of your year's formal curriculum.

This is an important point. There's so much to learn about reading and literature. You may well do a formal reading or writing lesson on how authors develop character. But you can also, any day of the year, ask students if they were particularly struck in that day's reading about how an author really let you know what a character was like, perhaps starting with such an "aha" moment in the book you were reading yourself that day. By the time you've completed a college education, you've read a lot of books and have a lot of lenses for understanding books. Learning about the lenses may well happen in classes where you learn about metaphor, plot structure, and so on, but it's in the actual reading — your whole life long — that you use the lenses and appreciate what they show you. The teacher's role in group sharing is in part to help students use those lenses, those literary appreciation tools, while in the midst of experiencing the books.

A Conference with Every Reader Every Week

Regular conferences with each reader were at the core of Jeannette Veatch's work (1964, 1978). She suggested five minutes per child, ideally twice a week, with many ideas about what to talk about during that time. I think individual conferences are the single most powerful tool that we have for the teaching of reading, and am surprised that so few teachers use them. I'll talk first about purposes and logistics, then about how to conduct them.

The purpose of an individual reading conference is to conduct regular assessment and teaching with every student in the class. It's not meant to be a milestone procedure, such as one conducted every time a kid finishes a book, but dipping a foot in the water of her reading to take its temperature. Given this, the best way to handle the logistics is with a regular conference schedule. At the beginning of the year, set aside (say) half an hour every day broken into five-minute time slots. Then give every student a time slot. They can choose them themselves, but why not just do it alphabetically, since it doesn't really matter? This sets up a routine that will help the whole process run smoothly, so that, say, Brianni will know to come to the teacher conference corner every Wednesday at 10:20.

Getting the logistics to run well also involves talking with the students about why you're doing it, and setting up a climate in which there's half an hour every day when the rest of the class is engaged in activities that don't require your presence. (They can be reading, or doing other activities or schoolwork.) When the student arrives at the conference, he should expect to bring a book that he's reading or has just finished and be ready to talk about it. The teacher doesn't need any preparation, other than perhaps looking back over notes from previous conferences with that student. She should, however, have a record-keeping system. I'd recommend either a loose-leaf notebook with a page for every student, or peel-off labels (2" × 3"?) that can be written on and then added to a student's file later. It's very important to document what goes on in the conferences, to be discussed further in Chapter 11.

The individual reading conference is a cross between a conversation with another reader and a lesson. The conversation part may begin the same way every time: "Hi, I see you're reading [insert name of book]. Tell me a little about it." You can then think of the conversation as a potential series of branching tracks, where the student's response prompts a low-key teaching move on your part. Student: "I'm really scared for the kids in *Roll of Thunder* because I think they might get into a lot of trouble." Teacher: "How does Mildred Taylor get you worried by hinting at the kinds of trouble they might get into?" In Chapter 6, I'll talk in more detail about components of individual conferences, but for now think of them as having a small number of brief segments: talking about the book, with a little teaching; the student reading aloud a bit for the information it gives you as the teacher; and establishing what's next for this reader — another book by the same author, a different genre, or what?

Also, is he ready to try a harder book? You then write a few lines of notes as this student leaves and the next one arrives. The conference thus achieves a personal contact with the student, as well as assessment, teaching, planning, and documentation. It should be brief but frequent. Five minutes a week for the thirty-five weeks of the school year gives you three hours a year of one-on-one time with each child; we surely need at least this much to ensure that all students have a reading connection with you, and that no one falls through the cracks.

What Else?

I tell prospective teachers that if you were to provide only reading time, sharing, and individual conferences, you'd have a respectable reading program in which students would progress. However, we want to do much more. Some teachers may have constraints like a mandated basal series or other program, or only a forty-five-minute period for English language arts. They may also have established readers' workshop programs that they're happy with and not need a full set of new ideas for their curriculum. The Common Core State Standards will also increasingly be entering the curriculum landscape. In Chapters 9 and 10 I provide a multitude of ideas, enough to encompass an entire support and teaching system on top of the independent reading itself. At this point, then, I'll say that the rest of the reading time, beyond the three components I've described, will vary, but is likely to include a mixture of connecting kids with books, teaching, and reading-related activities. I'd like to mention one other component, however, that we should be thinking about from the first day of school and on a daily basis.

Goals for Reading

At the beginning of the school year, once you've done your initial assessments and have the daily reading program up and running, talk with your students about their personal reading goals for the year. Thinking about reading goals should also be a yearlong process.

Begin with a conversation about students' goals for themselves, whether they have them, what they are. Young children are likely, of course, to need more scaffolding: perhaps "How are you different as a reader than when you finished first grade last year? What would you like to accomplish by the end of second grade?" Upper elementary kids can really get into meatier chapter books and nonfiction. Middle and high school students may have begun to think about career goals. If you have your own reading goals, or can set some, that's a good place to go next. In my case, I'd say, "Several years ago, I decided to make a New Year's resolution of reading two or three books a week. Some of my friends made fun of me for making a resolution to do something I wanted to do already, but it ended up getting me more focused on making time to read and finishing the books I started. Do you have any ideas for reading goals for this year? They could be about how many books you'd like to read, or what kind, or getting stronger as a reader to tackle a book that's too hard for you now."

If you're working with leveled books, you can talk to kids about criteria for how many levels students at their grade can be expected to rise, not as any kind of mandate but as a touchstone of increased maturity. (See Fountas and Pinnell, 2006.) Students who are reading novels and longer nonfiction books might think about numbers of books or pages per week, to help keep themselves focused. (Be clear that it's not about feeling compelled to meet volume goals every week or month but rather about having some in mind, just as an adult might aim to exercise a certain amount.) High school students might want to expand their reading into topics that will support their college and career directions after they graduate, for instance, seeking out memoirs by cops, physicians, or athletes. The goals might also involve time spent on reading; for instance, a total of seven hours a week outside of school.

It's important that students have a sense of ownership for these goals. They can be further refined and scaffolded in individual conferences, but they should begin from their own sense of what they see themselves doing and achieving over the course of the year. The goals can of course be modified if they turn out to be too modest or ambitious, or if their interests change. You can, however, insist that they have *some* goal for reading. To the kids who have no interest in reading, you can say, "This is school and it's my job to get you reading, but I can't do it without your participation. Here's my part: I'll do everything I can to make reading fun and interesting for you, and you get to read what you want. Your part, at this point, is to set some goals and start giving it a try."

The students can choose not to share their goals publicly, particularly if there are some who are embarrassed about not reading as well as their classmates. Special needs students and English language learners may need some support from you in goal setting. For instance, the goals for a newly arrived student from an African country whose language has no written form will be different than those for an American student with a reading disability.

As part of the discussion, I'd be sure to introduce the idea of volume of reading if it hasn't already come up. I'd share with them some information about how important it is. Using the number of books I introduced in Chapter 1 for each grade level, see how they sound to your students and ask whether they'd like to incorporate them in their goals. I'd strongly recommend that students write a dated entry in a reading journal about their goals for the year (and ideally, the teacher will set personal reading goals as well). You can suggest that they keep them on their minds, talk about them in class occasionally, and plan to review how their progress is coming along in a month or so. They don't need to talk about their goals all the time, but perhaps they can at least look at them occasionally. Changing them during the year is okay too.

We've now explored the key components of the reading curriculum, how to start off the year, and what the day will look like. The rest of this book fills out the details of everything else: how to promote reading more books and harder books by

1. making books available
2. getting kids reading if they don't know how yet
3. connecting kids with books
4. teaching in ways that make students stronger readers
5. documenting their learning.

Again, this isn't a generic how-to-teach-reading book but a series of teacher moves that will target volume and complexity.

6

Inspire Kids to Read and Match Them with Books

Now for the fun part: connecting your students with all those great books and the excitement they bring. And not just excitement, but laughter, tears, thinking, and wisdom. Think about the books that really stayed with you as a child, and about how many books there are for children to read and be moved by, and remember for the rest of their lives. You're the one who will make it happen.

Kids can learn about books from you, from the Internet and other resources, and from each other. Booktalks and read-alouds are the two main ways for your class to learn about books from you. Booktalks can be brief or more elaborate. Think of them as sales pitches. "Wow. The Newbery Awards were just announced and I realized we already have two of the Honor Books here in the classroom." "I just got another book by Steve Jenkins. I know how much you already love his collage artwork and facts about animals. This one looks at endangered species." "You might not know that Suzanne Collins wrote a series before *The Hunger Games*. Here it is!" Any of these could be expanded by talking about the subject matter of the book, who the author is, familiar books that it's similar to in some way, and so on. You might also choose a passage to read aloud.

Reading Aloud to Kids

For young students, reading aloud, particularly picture books that aren't easy reading, exposes them to books that they couldn't access on their own. And when a picture book has been read aloud to them, they can choose to look at it on their own later and will perhaps be able to read some of it. Later on in the elementary grades, reading entire novels aloud provides a shared literary experience (more about this in Chapter 10), and is best done with books that are a little more challenging in their content and themes than what students usually choose to read on their own. In addition to the scaffolding that you do to help them appreciate the read-aloud book itself, its greater sophistication may spur them to add more complex books to their personal reading. In middle school and high school, there's rarely time for reading aloud anymore, but a small amount of it can accompany a booktalk as an interest-builder, especially if the book starts off intriguingly.

Resources

Students can also be guided about how to get their own ideas of what books to read, particularly as they get older. Many of the resources you use yourself can also be used by kids; it's easy to provide links, for instance, to online sources, such as those for the major award winners, and to print out annotated listings such as the *New York Times'* list of about a dozen best children's books each year, categorized by grade range. These days, most children's authors have websites aimed at their readers. Nancie Atwell's students' booklists, mentioned in Chapter 2, are constantly updated, and have the advantage of being created by kids. You can also help students do web searches for bibliographies of children's books of particular types.

Sharing

Students' own recommendations to each other are also extremely valuable. You can increase the power of kids' peer recommendations by providing as many venues for them as possible, all of them easy to set up: sharing time during readers' workshop; planned and somewhat more formal oral book reviews; book groups for students who want to discuss a book they've all read; comments on the classroom's LibraryThing page; a database of student-written book reviews (possibly published online); and a regularly printed book review newspaper, perhaps circulated to audiences beyond their own classroom. What's especially useful here isn't just a sense of whether students think a particular book is good, but what exactly they liked about it and what kinds of readers it would appeal to. The teacher can build on peer recommendation by suggesting other books not only by the same author but of the same type.

Conferences

The teacher's role becomes even more important in matching particular readers with particular books. The primary tool for doing this is the individual reading conference. For students to read enough books and hard-enough books, teacher guidance is crucial. Note that this is guidance, not mandates. A few years ago, I asked sixth-grade boys on a panel at a children's literature conference what, in their view, was most important for teachers to know about their reading. One of the three items they mentioned was "Don't make us read stuff we don't want to." (The other two were to have books in the genres they like, and to let them do nonboring things to respond to their books.) Many, many students have been turned off to reading at some point in their school careers because of mandated books. (Personally, in high school I hated *Arrowsmith*, by Sinclair Lewis, which we did as a class book.[1] Interestingly, nobody reads it anymore, so what was the point?)

This guidance in helping students find the right books for them is especially crucial as the Common Core State Standards are implemented more and more widely. The Publishers' Criteria for the Standards for grades 3–12, which will be used to develop curriculum materials, explicitly say, "Texts for each grade align with the complexity requirements outlined in the standards." However, reading texts at the standards-established level should *never* be more than a minor goal. If such curriculum materials become the entire reading program, many students will be mandated, and perhaps limited, to reading material that's often appreciably too hard for them. Even the best teaching can't make this work. The *core* of students' reading is the books that they're interested in; part of what characterizes those books is that they're at the appropriate complexity level for the *kid*, not the grade. Students are the best judges of the complexity level that's best for them, with teachers working to ensure that they're not just coasting with easy books. We'll return to the topic of reading harder books, but this chapter is about leading and mentoring kids to the right books for them.

Questions for Students

In helping students choose their own reading through conferences, focus on a few key topics. First, do you like the book you're reading now, and is it a "just-right" book? This presumes that your class understands what's been called the Goldilocks principle (see Wikipedia): we're generally happiest reading books that are comfortable in their difficulty level (and stretching a little bit), although we sometimes relax with an easier book or challenge ourselves with a harder one. Second, what thoughts do you have about what to read next? Something similar, or something different? A

---

[1] There is, however, a role for whole-class books, which I'll talk about later.

book that's been recommended or that you saw mentioned? Or would you like some suggestions? Third, are you ready to stretch a little on your next book? It's especially valuable to time the asking of this question based on knowing what the student has been reading for the last month or so. Has she just moved into books without illustrations, and needs some time to get comfortable with them? Have all the young adult novels she's been reading been on the short side? Is she on a kick of reading nonfiction about Egypt and maybe ready for a novel?

Conversations

Individual conferences are the avenue for fine-tuning the connecting of individual readers with particular books, but it can also be supported through whole-class conversations. For instance, you could do a lesson on "how we found some of the best books we've read." This can start with a personal anecdote about how you read a review of a book, or heard about it from a friend, and just had a feeling that you were going to like it: the story sounded really interesting, or it was a chance to learn more about a topic you'd always wondered about, or it sounded like it was written in a style that would really engage you. The focus is mainly to get kids thinking about keeping their eyes and ears open for clues that a particular book might be right for them.

Strategies for Book Choice

Another lesson could be about strategies for choosing a book, perhaps if a student's trying to decide between several new books in the classroom library. The book jacket or paperback cover, as well as (sometimes) pages at the very beginning or end of the book, provide a lot of information: a summary of the story or content, usually written in a way that tries to entice you into reading the book (or buying it if you're in a store); blurbs by other authors; quotes from reviews; any awards it's received or "best book" lists it's been on; information about the author, including previous books; and the publication date. (The book cover design is of course what you notice first, but it's mainly a marketing tool that's not necessarily a useful guide to whether you'll like the book.) Reading the first page of the book is also a good strategy, as well as flipping through to get a general sense of how it's written.

Stick with It or Not?

Another lesson is about how long to stick with a book before giving up on it. It's often good to give a book a try if there's reason to think that you might like it, even if it doesn't draw you in at first, but you also need to be free to give up on it if it just isn't working for you. There's no magic rule or number of pages, but it's worth discussing and thinking about. (One of my favorite books ever is one that I couldn't get into at first but then was stuck with on a long bus trip with nothing else to read; I've also abandoned novels twenty pages from the end when I realized that I just didn't care what happened.) Readers might develop personal rules of thumb, such as "give it fifteen minutes, but more if it's come highly recommended," or if it seems at all promising. Or give yourself time to get into it even if it seems hard. Or if you're getting confused by all the characters, make a list of them to keep yourself oriented. If students have e-readers, they can usually download a sample chapter to read before buying a book. But a reader can always choose to abandon a book, at any point.

Harder Books

One more lesson about choosing books is about the value of ramping it up and moving into harder books. This should be part of the ongoing classroom conversation all year, of course, beginning with the discussion of goals early on, but it's also useful to focus on it specifically. I'd begin by inviting students to talk about a time they remember that they chose to read a book that was a little harder than one they'd read before. (This could range from their first chapter book to their first move from young adult into adult fiction.) What made you decide to do it? How did you know this book was going to be harder? What was rewarding about it? What if anything was hard about it? Were you happy you'd read it?

Then move into a discussion (in an age-appropriate way, depending on the grade level) about the importance of reading harder stuff as part of the path to maturity. As you grow older, the books you read when you were younger will bore you (aside from an occasional foray into nostalgia). Your world expands, and the books you read will expand too. It's not just that the words, sentences, and books themselves get bigger and longer; the ideas get bigger, the characters get deeper. Part of how this happens is through readers pushing themselves into reading books that are a little bit harder than what they're reading already (with the teacher as cheerleader), not totally too hard to read at all, but a little challenging. Every time you take on a slightly harder book, you become a slightly stronger reader. This doesn't happen with every new book you choose, but you can see it happen over the course of a school year. That's one reason it's so valuable to keep a list of all the books you read; you can see how far you've come. You can usually tell if a book is a bit of a stretch for you; also, if you know you're reading level P, level Q is probably a good bet for a stretch. For older students, transitioning from young adult to adult books and from shorter to longer books are ways of stretching. You can also decide that a book you've decided to try is indeed a bit too hard, and put it aside to try again in a couple of months. (Much of the ability to read more complex texts comes, of course, from the reading itself, but I'll talk later about the important role of teaching in making this reading growth happen.)

Expanding Choices

There are a few special circumstances to consider in matching readers with books. First, as mentioned earlier, what about English language learners whose English isn't strong enough yet to read the books they'd otherwise be interested in? Should they be encouraged to read in their own language even if they aren't yet fully or at all literate in it? Yes, if possible, and then the teacher can also gradually help them move to reading more and more in English as their knowledge of it increases. This way at least some of their literacy can be at their own intellectual level. Also, just as with struggling readers who can't yet read material that's content-appropriate for them, you should ensure that the classroom library has high-interest, easy-reading materials for English language learners who are still transitioning.

Similarly, students may really, really want to read specific books that are age-appropriate but still too hard for them. This is especially painful if everyone else is reading the latest hot series books and a few kids are unable to read them independently. In these cases, it's well worth investing in audiobooks, often available from libraries. They're especially useful if you encourage students to follow along with the written text in the book as they listen, so that the audio isn't standing on its own but providing scaffolding for the written text. Some ebook readers offer an audio option; it may be spoken mechanically rather than read fluently, but that can be good enough.

Another question that teachers often ask is about the student whose range of reading is quite narrow, such as all one genre, or the complete works of one author, or only nonfiction. Should they be required to mix it up and read more broadly? In a word, no. This can be very hard for teachers to accept, and certainly teachers should expose students to all types of literature. But if we want to accomplish the goal of reading more books and harder books, the choice needs to remain with the reader, particularly if we're going for high volume. We can encourage kids to expand their horizons, and suggest specific books that might be somewhat outside of their current interests, and I think it's even appropriate during the course of a genre study to ask all students to, for instance, include one play in their reading. But the vast majority of what students read has to be self-selected, just as you can't force children to eat food that they really just don't like. Also, reading deeply is at least as good as reading broadly.

Another way to think about this is to realize that the English language arts curriculum has multiple goals. One of them is to expose students to a wide variety of literature, and I'll talk at the end of this chapter about whether there should be a canon of some kind for what all American students should read, which our schools especially encourage for high school. But what's most important is that young people read a lot and read harder books as they go along, and this just can't happen if they aren't choosing the books themselves. We have to be supportive guides, not controllers of what students read. We can still have a rich literature curriculum, in the sense of seeing literature as a full content area, just like history, but it doesn't mean that everything students read has to be in the service of the literature curriculum.

Students who don't want to read very much or at all, or who aren't willing to stretch into harder books, are a different matter. This would be (I'm exaggerating!) like a young child who wasn't just saying "I don't like carrots" but refusing to eat at all, or refusing to move beyond Gerber's to solid food. These are the students for whom your most important job is to help them figure out what reading has to offer them. There are a variety of reasons why kids are reluctant readers (listed here in a rough sequence, starting with those more likely to be seen at younger ages): minimal previous exposure to books; just not ready to read yet; more interested in active than quiet pursuits; unable to read, possibly because of a learning disability; ashamed about being unable to read or not proficient enough; haven't found anything they want to read; previous negative experiences with reading and reading instruction; burned out on school. Sometimes acting oppositional or defiant about reading can be a mask for shame or embarrassment.

Your job as the teacher is to figure out what's going on and work with the student in a way that's consistent with the root causes. This is likely to include some combination of exploring her interests, teaching her how to read, suggesting books that are both age- and reading-level-appropriate, and generally making it fun. Can you insist that they read? Well, yes and no. You can establish an expectation that reading is part of the life of your classroom, and that everybody needs to have a book in front of them during reading time. But you can't force someone to read, since it's a cognitive process, and assigning "consequences" if they don't read doesn't help create avid, lifelong readers. I suggest that we think of accountability in a different way than schools often do. Rather than saying that a student is accountable to do a certain amount of reading, why not say that *we're* the ones who are accountable, to her and her family, to get her reading using everything we can to make it appealing and possible for her. The fewer strictures the better: if she's able to spend a couple of months reading cartoon books, she may be more likely to read novels later than if we'd force-fed them to her in the first place.

Appropriate Choices?

Speaking of cartoon books: I'd like to speak here to the question of issues of appropriateness when students are choosing their own reading. I'll consider three dimensions of the topic: "subliterature," controversial children's and young adult books, and truly inappropriate material. Subliterature is a mildly derogatory term that can be used to refer to genre fiction such as mysteries and romances. It was often used in the past, particularly by children's librarians, to refer to comic books, joke books, series books, and other material designed for children but not considered very worthwhile. Magazines may also fall into this category, particularly those dealing with popular topics like sports, motorcycles, and gaming. Teachers sometimes feel that kids should be reading good-quality literature in school. However, this idea is generally misguided. Voracious adult readers often read all of this stuff as children, and it's especially useful for weaker and reluctant readers.

Series books are great for building fluency. Their predictability, which eventually becomes boring, is useful when you're still figuring out reading; for instance, you don't have to get to know all new characters in every book. Comic books have, of course, also morphed into the rich and respected genre of stories, novels, and nonfiction in graphic format, a great addition to the world of literature. Magazines can also be considered a genre, distinctive for their timeliness, and valuable throughout adult life. The only concern with these materials is if students stay stuck in them as their only reading material, particularly little cartoon and joke books that don't have much text or coherent idea development, or magazines where pictures are the major draw for kids. Struggling readers may need support to move into more complex reading.

Many teachers wonder about having books in their classrooms that are definitely intended for children but may have mature themes, rough language, and sexual content. Every year, schools and libraries face challenges to these books, to the extent that both NCTE and the American Library Association have suggested policies for dealing with them. Some school libraries were unwilling to order *The Higher Power of Lucky*, 2007's Newbery Medal winner, because the word *scrotum* appeared on the first page. (The author, Susan Patron, a public librarian herself, offered a powerful defense of this choice in an NPR interview; www.npr.org/templates/story/story.php?storyId=7644587.) If students are choosing their own books, there are concerns that some of those books may be problematic because the teacher won't have oversight of them. The best answer to this question is to let the children's and young adult literature community be your guide. When a book has been 1) marketed to young audiences; 2) well reviewed by a source such as *Horn Book* or *Publishers' Weekly*, and 3) acquired by a library for the children's or young adult shelves, that's adequate vetting. These books may include many that would be uncomfortable as a whole-class book but are excellent for children to read on their own, such as Judy Blume's classic, *Deenie*, about a young girl with scoliosis, that includes a brief masturbation scene. It would be icky to read aloud and discuss in class, but fine as a personal choice for its intended readers. When books are truly inappropriate, particularly adult books with strong sexual themes, students know it. You won't have them in your classroom library, and if kids bring them in, it's enough to say, "That book isn't appropriate for school," and, (just like we all did as teenagers), they'll read them privately.

Kids Picking Their Own Books for Class Reading

I'd like to finish this chapter on matching students with books with a brief discussion on whether there are some books that all students should read. E. D. Hirsch's controversial book *Cultural Literacy* (1987) included a famous list of information, including literature, that all Americans should be familiar with, from *Alice in Wonderland* and Antigone to *Wuthering Heights* and Emile Zola. Hirsch went on to develop a set of brief encyclopedias and the Core Knowledge Foundation to further promulgate his ideas. The Common Core State Standards have more recently raised issues of what, if anything, all students should be reading. (According to them, the list should include foundational documents from American history, such as Thomas Paine's *Common Sense*, which I confess I've never read.) The National Council of Teachers of English (NCTE) hasn't supported the idea of a literature canon for some time. But should we think about including some common books for everyone as part of reading more books and reading harder books? Also, should "everyone" be defined nationally, or by states, districts, or schools?

Here are some thoughts on the topic, not intended to be definitive but rather to provoke discussion. I'll focus just on fiction here and leave the question of essential informational texts to the content areas. Most teachers will want to include some whole-class books, and most teachers, particularly in high school, think it's valuable for students to read some classics. Could it be useful for teachers to set up lists of multiple books, contemporary and classic, and think about using them in a variety of ways? Several years ago, in a class for prospective high school teachers, I gave them the following list of books in the form of a bracket list like the one used in tournaments. (I got the idea from the book *The Final Four of Everything*, 2009.[2]) The list is one possible one; similar ones could be made for other age levels.

1. Alexie, *The Absolutely True Diary of a Part-Time Indian* (or equivalent by Young Adult author of color)
2. Austen, *Pride and Prejudice*
3. *Beowulf*
4. Book groups—students pick from a choice of four or so books from recent ALA Young Adult Top Ten lists
5. Ellison, *Invisible Man* (or equivalent adult novel by a contemporary American author of color)
6. Fitzgerald, *The Great Gatsby*
7. Hawthorne, *The Scarlet Letter*
8. Hinton, *The Outsiders*
9. Lee, *To Kill a Mockingbird*
10. Printz Award winner for Young Adult literature (your choice)
11. Saramago, *Blindness* (or another Nobel Prize winner in translation)
12. Shakespeare, your choice
13. Steinbeck, *Of Mice and Men*
14. Twain, *Huckleberry Finn*
15. Wilson, a play from the "Pittsburgh cycle"
16. Your pick (a book you'd like to teach)

I invited them to talk about these titles in small groups as if they were tournament brackets, choosing one book over the other in each pair as the one they'd more like to teach, and narrowing it down until they had picked the one book they absolutely

---

[2] By the way, a similar bracketology tournament recently chose *The Wire* as the best TV series ever.

would choose to use as a whole-class book in their classroom. It was, of course, the discussion that mattered rather than the results.

Wouldn't it be fun to create, perhaps with some colleagues, a list of sixteen books, classic and contemporary, that would be valuable for your grade level, and then present the list to your students? The idea would be for them to look at the books, listen to booktalks on them, and see which ones they'd like to explore as a whole class (thus the tournament format), and whether it would also be fun to read as many as possible as part of their personal reading. (Remember that you'd do a *few* class books, and that any other reading of all sixteen would be purely as an optional part of students' much larger personal reading choices.) This is similar to the Young Reader's Choice Awards established by a number of states and regions, where students are invited to read from a list of nominated books and send in their votes. I believe this would be an especially valuable activity for middle grades and up, where students are reading fewer books than they did in first and second grade, and it would be easy to assemble lists for students to choose from. We'd have many of the benefits of a canon, but one that could be locally appropriate and frequently updated, and still keep the element of personal choice of what to read. There'd be enough buzz about the books (I think sixteen is a good number) that students would become familiar with all of them. It's also very easy to find lists of 100 best children's or young adult books online to make your selections from (although those that are crowd-sourced tend to include less recent books). You might also enjoy *1001 Children's Books You Must Read Before You Grow Up* (2009), which covers ages 0–12+. (Note that it's British, with coverage somewhat different from what an American version would include.)

7

A Community of Readers

tudents' book recommendations are an avenue for them to learn about books from each other. This community of readers can also be a tool for further teaching and learning. The official (that is, my) mantra for this is No. Book. Reports. No cutesy alternatives to book reports either: writing a different ending to the story, writing a letter to the character, making a shoebox diorama of the book's setting. (Well, maybe dioramas in some cases; read on!) We all hated book reports as kids, and we all know that the major purpose for them was to make sure the kid had read the book. This continues even in college children's literature classes. Decades ago, I dropped the idea of having college students turn in annotated bibliographies of the children's books they'd read; plain bibliographies allowed them more time for reading, and students of any age can cheat on annotations and book reports. If you have a rich readers' workshop, you'll know the students have read the books from your conferences with them and everything else that goes on in class.

However, there are plenty of ways for students to respond authentically to what they've read, and they're best done in the context of a classroom community. Books about teaching children's literature are full of these (see especially Bedford and Albright, 2011, for fresh ideas). I'd like to suggest a framework for incorporating them into the mix of reading and teaching.

First, small-group discussions of books. The model here is the adult book club, where readers decide to read a book in common and discuss it. In the classroom, book clubs are often referred to as literature circles. In some cases they've become perhaps overly codified, with defined roles for each student and specific tasks, but you can think of them as taking a variety of different forms, depending on several parameters.

One example: a group of students can decide to read the same book (perhaps from several suggested by the teacher) and discuss it on a set date. The discussion might be completely open-ended, or the teacher could suggest some guiding questions. Appleman (2006) wrote about her experience doing this outside of class time with high school students over the course of a year. In a different model, first-graders who can't read yet could be invited to sit in groups; each group would look at an unfamiliar picture book in detail. You'd ask that every child say something about the pictures on each two-page spread, followed by whole-class sharing. (Obviously, you'll choose books where the pictures tell much if not all of the story.) In a sixth-grade biography unit, students who are reading biographies of different people can meet regularly as they read their books; a teaching point could be giving them one focus question every time they meet, such as thinking about the author's choice of chapter titles, or the extent to which the subject's childhood is explored in the book.

Students can also form their own book groups, which can be incorporated into a general literacy time in the classroom day. These could be focused on a book, an author, a theme, and so on. The teacher's role is primarily to spark the idea, but then also to suggest focus questions appropriate to what they're reading. Students have ownership of the group, but the teacher can be its coach. Often, when students are all in their book groups, the best role of the teacher can be to kibitz: move from one group to another, chiming in with thoughts or questions that seem appropriate.

The values of book groups are many: they move reading from a solitary activity to its being a social one as well; they can deepen your understanding of that particular book, particularly if it's one that's a little bit challenging; they can help students understand how to look more analytically at a book, but with peers rather than a teacher's instruction; they can help readers think and talk about a book with the book open in front of them to clarify understanding; with many books, they can help students and their peers connect reading with their own lives.

A second avenue for creating a classroom community of readers is through invitations (Short, Harste, and Burke, 1996), where you provide ways of responding in a variety of media to the books you've read, not as assignments but as choices. These are especially appropriate in elementary school, but need not be limited to those years. In invitations, the teacher suggests, teaches about, and facilitates writing, art, and media responses to literature for those students who are interested. A simple example for primary grades: "Let's make a bulletin board of some of our favorite characters in the books we're reading. If you're interested in planning this, sign up to meet at the art table at 10:30 during literacy time today." The committee would then decide how to organize the bulletin board and invite the rest of the class to make cut-out characters to their specifications. In fifth grade, students could be invited to act out and videotape scenes from the book their literature study group is reading. For those who still love shoebox dioramas, you could set up a center (particularly appropriate when you're focusing on the role of setting in books) with materials for them and a brief tutorial session. It's the difference between "Today we're all going to make dioramas of our books" (ugh!) and "Here's a way to represent your book artistically that some of you might enjoy." A group of older students involved in a biography-reading unit might enjoy using what they've learned about how biographies are structured to write a biography for younger audiences that they can self-publish and place in a lower-grade classroom library. The key to invitations is that they create *voluntary* and optional ways for students to respond together to books in engaging ways.

A third tool of the community of readers is for students to share their thoughts about the books they've read within and beyond their own classroom. A very simple structure involves having a class LibraryThing.com page to catalog all of the books that everyone in the class has read. Then when new books come in or students read books they get elsewhere, they're added in. Its use in the classroom community is for students to add comments that anyone can refer to after they've read a book. . This will, of course, work best if you discuss first what kinds of comments are most useful. You can also decide to use, for instance, a four-star ranking system in the comments. Example of a good comment: four stars, because the plot really moved along and I was surprised by some of what happened. Example of a less useful comment: three stars, I liked it because it was good.

You can also go more formal with students' reactions by having them write book reviews for real audiences. To do this right, you'll want to help them understand what real book reviews look like. Book reviews are of course a genre of (usually short) informational/critical writing, and students can learn about the genre in age-appropriate ways. For younger students unable to read published reviews of the books they read (since the reviews are written for adults), you can teach a lesson about what a good book review should include: some information about what the book is about (but no detailed plot summaries or spoilers, please!), what makes it special or distinguishes it from other books, and how good you think it is and why. Older students can of course read longer reviews (the *New York Times* has its complete archive online), and may be interested in learning about the kinds of long-form book reviews that occur in journals like *The New York Review of Books* and *Bookforum*. Then thinking about audience is crucial: it can start within the classroom, move to hallway bulletin boards, and be formalized as a regular publication to circulate to other classrooms or on a classroom blog. Once students have learned how to write good book reviews, some of them may choose to edit a classroom publication of reviews, or you might invite the first reader of a new book to write a review of it.

These ideas for seeing students as part of a community of readers should serve them well in their development. They'll have an audience beyond the teacher for their thoughts about books, and help each other become more sophisticated in their understanding, including helping each other move into harder books.

CHAPTER 8

Special Cases:
Beginning Readers, English Language Learners, Struggling Readers, Reluctant Readers

A n independent reading program needs kids who know how to read. If you teach first grade, getting them reading is obviously a big part of your job, but other, older students may not be reading yet either. Beginning reading is obviously a big enough topic to have its own book, but I'd like to use just this chapter to lay out a simple three-part plan to get all children quickly to the point where they can pick up books and read them on their own. It'll be relatively easy for the majority of first-graders, but there are also three other groups who may not be reading at all at a later age. For English language learners, becoming literate is often coupled to some extent with learning English, and they need appropriate support and, when possible, literacy in their first language. Every case is different, depending on how new they are to English, how similar their first language is to English, their age, and so on. Special needs students vary widely, but many of them are likely to need more time and more teacher support to learn how to read, in first grade or later. Older students who aren't yet able to read independently may fall into one or both of the first categories as well, and need to be treated with respect and care because of the self-esteem issues that affect older nonreaders. The basic teaching ideas are the same for all learners, but some are less likely to figure out reading at the same time as the rest of their classmates and will need more scaffolding at whatever age you meet them.

Connecting with Students' Previous Experiences

The process of initial reading instruction needs to build on what children know about written language before they come to school, taking into account differences in their background experiences. (For older nonreaders, we also need to think about their experiences with literacy during their previous years of school.) We know that children don't come to literacy as blank slates. (Baghban, 1984, and Harste, Woodward, and Burke, 1984, are two important examples of scholarship on the topic.) Children see written language in the world around them. In most cases they see people reading and writing in their daily lives and are likely to have experience with books and other written media. Some will also have preschool experience with literacy. This is all grounded in a foundation of oral language, which all children use with an amazing level of competence by the time they start school, in some cases in more than one language (Goodman, 1996). In a brief addendum to this chapter, I've described three important research studies that teachers working with children from different American cultures should be aware of in order to understand how these early experiences of language and literacy may vary.

Early discussions and conferences with beginning readers can focus on discovering what they know about print out in the world, what books are and how they work, and who they see reading and for what purposes. You'll also be aware of students' oral language, although some of it may be in a language other than your own, and special needs students may have language disabilities. It's important to realize, too, that speakers of all versions of American English have full language capacity, and that features that may seem "wrong" to you just reflect the language they've learned as part of their home community.

You can build on all of this in age- and situation-appropriate ways. Children need exposure to, and chances to use, a lot of oral language to further develop in ways that support reading. For English language learners, this of course means opportunities to use English while maintaining their home language. Focusing more directly on literacy involves forms and functions of literacy: exploring environmental print, looking at websites, writing lists and letters, and so on. For first graders, lots of exposure to books is crucial, through read-alouds and looking and talking about them on their own, especially if their earlier exposure to books has been limited.

For students in the other categories, you'll want to figure out what will be most important to build on in their individual cases to get them into reading. For the English language learner, you'll want to figure out the extent to which you'll be able to connect beginning literacy to their first language. For special needs students, it'll be valuable to get a sense of how they think and feel about books and reading, perhaps connecting them with age-appropriate picture books to get the fun of appreciating them even if they can't read them themselves yet. The older, perhaps reading-defiant student may benefit from taking the pressure off and having full agency over what kinds of reading materials you use with her. Obviously, each of these groups of students deserves a whole book of ideas about how to develop their literacy. (See Cary, 2007; Allington, 2009 and 2012; and Smith and Wilhelm, 2002, respectively.) But my point here is to tune in to whatever it is they're bringing to the process of learning to read, and realize that they're not empty vessels.

Predictable Books and Beyond

Most teachers are familiar with the gradual release-of-responsibility model: read-aloud; shared reading; guided reading; independent reading (developed originally by Meek, 1987, and Pearson and Gallagher, 1983, and since widely disseminated). Teachers are also familiar with predictable and other easy books, particularly using the early Guided Reading levels. Here's why this is such a powerful model, as documented by Margaret Moustafa in her brief, brilliant book *Beyond Traditional Phonics* (1997). When you read an easy, predictable book aloud to young children, particularly with repeated readings, they're likely to remember much of its language. A classic, familiar example is *Brown Bear, Brown Bear, What Do You See?* by Bill Martin, Jr. and Eric Carle. It repeats a pattern throughout, addressing one animal of one color and continuing on to speak to another animal of another color. Since the text is fully supported by the illustrations, listeners quickly become familiar with the text.

You then move quickly to shared reading, distinguished by the children's attending to the print on the page and chiming in as you read the text together, provided by an oversized book, screen, or multiple small copies. The process continues with guided reading of increasingly harder books, where the children read with teacher guidance and support; throughout, they'll eventually be able to read unfamiliar books on their own. (Guided reading in particular will still continue after students are reading independently.) Attention to the print is reinforced throughout by pointing to each word while reading, inviting children to find particular words, making sentence strips for children to put in order without picture support, and so on, as well as helping them realize that once a book has been read to or with a group, any one of them can pick it up and try it on her own.

The details of how to carry out this approach are more than I have space for here and will be familiar to or unnecessary for many of you; perhaps the most detailed handbook is *Guided Reading* (Fountas & Pinnell, 1996); look also for books specifically focused on first-grade reading (e.g., the short *First Grade Readers*, Parsons, 2010). But here's what we know about how and why it works. As children are exposed to large numbers of easy predictable books (think Guided Reading level A), they begin to pick up sight words. As they develop a large repertoire of them, they become able to recognize new words that recombine the parts of words they already know. Basically, after a while, if you can read *big* and *sack*, you can read *back*. (The parts that are recombined are the onset, the part of a syllable that occurs before the vowel, and the rime, the vowel and what follows it: Moustafa, 1997.) These are the parts we naturally rearrange in Pig Latin, where *big* becomes *ig-bay* and *sleep* becomes *eep-slay*. Voilà; most kids are reading, these days often by the end of kindergarten and certainly in first grade.

Supporting Children's Attention to Print and the Grapho-Phonic System

Beginning reading is supported by children's existing use of the sound system (phonetics), grammatical system (syntax), and meaning system (semantics) of language, whether for English, another language, or more than one language.[1] Children also, of course, as mentioned earlier, have knowledge of the written language of the world around them (with the exception of remote rural areas, particularly in third-world countries). What's new in learning to read is the relationship between written and spoken language, and in particular sounds and letters (for alphabetic languages like English). Teachers support this through a variety of teaching and activities. Most important are learning the alphabet, the names of the letters and what they look like; writing with invented spelling; and working with word families. I've written about all of these at length (see especially Wilde, 1992, 1997; a brief discussion here will help you understand what these are about, but see longer resources available for more detail.

Learning what the letters of the alphabet look like, and what their names are, gives children the visual information and vocabulary they need to begin their literate lives, and their knowledge of them should be assessed at the beginning of kindergarten and first grade. The best resource I've seen for learning the alphabet naturally is the

---

[1] It works somewhat differently for nonalphabetic languages.

article "*K* is Kristen's" (McGee and Richgels, 1989), which contains a great collection of strategies, including alphabet books and games; it need not take long. Once children know the names of the letters, they can write with invented spelling, in kindergarten for most children and certainly from the beginning of first grade, with appropriate scaffolding. Invented spelling isn't only a tool for independent writing, it's the most user-friendly way of developing knowledge about phonemic awareness (isolating the sounds of language) and phonics (letter/sound relationships). For English language learners it'll be useful to know something about the sound system of their home language, and its writing system if they're literate in it.

Working with word families helps bring children's developing knowledge of letters and sounds in words, particularly onset/rime patterns, into conscious awareness. At early levels it consists of lessons where children think of words starting with the same sound, as the teacher writes them for children to see: ranging from single-letter onsets (big/bat/baby) to digraphs (cheese/chip/child) to blends (black/blue/blood). Then as children are beginning to read, move on to a single rime with varied onsets (slip/hip/dip). You can help them realize that they can use their knowledge of patterns like this when they come to a word they don't know, and try it out with some nonsense words: *shoop* starts like *shoe* and ends like *loop*, so you can read it even if it's not a real word. There's no need to explore every possible word family (my advice: skip the -*uck* family); it's about the process of being able to come up with a pronunciation of an unknown word (along with your sense of what word would fit the context) and loses much of its usefulness with words longer than one syllable.

Allington and McGill-Franzen (2012) commented recently that we have the knowledge to get all children reading quickly, and the plan I've just described is much of how to do so. Once readers have become able to pick up an unfamiliar book and read it on their own (with the supports of shared and guided reading, along with one-on-one assistance when they're almost there), they're ready to begin high-volume independent reading with books of their own choice, moving forward through leveled books. Although I haven't singled it out directly, making meaning from what they read is crucial and primary at every point along this path. We're not talking about word-calling but about *really* reading. Talking about books and reading conferences are important ways to make sure this is happening.

At this point in development, guided reading groups and individual conferences are still crucial to keep the early reading on track, and children may want and need to read books multiple times to build confidence, fluency, and speed, but they'll no longer need intensive scaffolding, and we can move on to more sophisticated teaching, as explored in Chapter 8. (Remember, scaffolding for buildings, the source of the metaphor, only stays up until the building can stand on its own.) For most native-English-speaking children, beginning to read around first grade, this all happens pretty easily.

A few more thoughts about the kinds of support that children who are slower to begin reading, and older students who can't yet read independently, may need. (English language learners are often becoming literate and learning English at the same time; if they can read in another language with the same alphabet, the literacy part is already in place and just needs to be adapted to a perhaps different mapping of letter/sound relationships.) With a student who isn't yet reading when other students are, a number of questions need to be considered. Younger children (ages five to six) may just not be quite ready yet, or may have had fewer literacy-related experiences before starting school, an especially relevant issue in communities of poverty, of course, perhaps especially rural ones with less exposure and access to print. Children of any age vary, and any individual child may fall somewhere on one or more special needs spectrums, so that literacy just comes harder to them. Older nonreaders may have fallen through the cracks in their earlier years of school or be resistant to reading, and are likely to feel shame and a need for secrecy about not reading.

What they need, however, is the same thing that all beginning readers need: an understanding on your part of the role of literacy in their life before they met you; repeated reading of predictable books; and attention to the grapho-phonic system.

Two books by Richard Allington (2009, 2012) are the best detailed resources available. But here's a short version that really just involves variations on the three earlier themes: 1) Get to know the student and her literacy as it exists at this moment in time. This part may take a while, and includes developing trust, exploring interests, and working to establish her sense of what role literacy could play in her life: hopes and dreams, really. With older students, it's important to be really patient, and consider yourself accountable for searching for the key that will unlock the literacy door for her. You can't control the outcome, but you can do all the right moves: Is there someone in your family who reads a lot? Is there something you'd like to learn more about? What could I do better than your other reading teachers did? 2) Find stuff to read. In some cases, have the student tell or dictate stories that then become the text for his reading. (Freire, 1970, developed this method for adults, and Lee, Van Allen, and Lamoreaux, 1963, among others, for children.) Get audiobooks that he can listen to while following along in the text visually. Get comics, graphic novels, cartoon books, easy but nonbabyish nonfiction, and relatively easy newspapers like *USA Today*, or whatever else works for your students. 3) Use the gradual release-of-responsibility method one-on-one, and explore letter/sound relationships through invented spelling and work with word families. The methods of the Reading Recovery program (Clay, 1993, and others) work well.

Often the most important thing to know about late starters, special needs students, and English language learners is that they need more one-on-one support to begin reading; for whatever reasons, they may not pick up an idea from a class lesson and will need the back-and-forth that personalized teaching can offer. This is the reason we have extra funding sources such as Title I; most children largely teach themselves how to read given the right experiences; however, the others are an example of the 80/20 rule (the Pareto Principle): 20 percent of the kids need 80 percent of the teacher's time. Let's help it happen as fast as it can, then get them reading independently like everyone else.

Addendum: Three Important Studies About the Influence of Culture and Poverty in Becoming Literate

First, *Ways with Words* (Heath, 1983) was a deep ethnographic look at literacy in two poor- to working-class southern communities, one white and one black, also contrasting them with middle-class culture of both races. Heath found that there were subtle but important differences between the communities. For instance, the African American community valued being able to tell a good story, while the working-class whites often saw telling stories as "lying" (for largely religious reasons). When the children from these communities arrived at school, their ways of using language didn't always mesh with school culture. For instance, the African American child in first grade, when asked "What's the animal in that picture?" would be thinking "Doesn't the teacher know that's a cow?" because in his world you don't ask questions you already know the answer to. The big takeaway idea from this book is that if teachers are working with children from a culture other than their own, they need to really "get it" about how to build on the language and literacy that's already comfortable for those children. There's no quick list of what this involves, but often a staff-room conversation about "what I don't understand about these kids is ..." can be a signal that cultural difference may be involved.

Other People's Words (Purcell-Gates, 1995) is a moving case study of a young working-class boy whose family was transplanted from Appalachia and living in Cincinnati. His family's history of literacy was limited; not only was he not successfully learning to read, Purcell-Gates worked with his mother to develop her literacy as well. An example of the mother's lack of experience came on their visit to the main public library, less than a mile from their home. She was stunned at the number of books, and that you could choose books to take home for free. This book clearly shows that if literacy isn't part of children's lives outside of school, we need to help them develop lives in which reading occurs. In this case there were also gender issues; the boy's father had no use for reading, so his son didn't see it as a "guy" thing to do.

Finally, *Meaningful Differences in the Everyday Experience of Young American Children* (Hart and Risley, 1995) documents a lengthy study of early language development with forty-two families of different social classes. Their major finding was that children's vocabulary size at the age of 36 months varied widely, with social class being the most influential variable. Every child grew up with good parents in caring families, but the welfare families simply used less language with their children. This study involved a small number of cases in one community in Iowa, and certainly can't be taken as predictive of poor children's vocabulary development in general, but it is a wake-up call to realize that, although all children will come to school with perfectly adequate vocabularies for the demands of everyday life, vocabulary development, much of it through reading, and starting at the beginning of schooling, is crucial to ensuring academic success for all students, and that we especially need to attend to intense vocabulary growth for children of poverty.

I'd recommend reading all three of these books if the topics interest you; I've hardly done them justice in a paragraph each. But they offer three big ideas for getting beginning reading going, especially if we want to achieve high-volume reading for all students and prevent achievement gaps as they go through the years of school. First, language and literacy practices at home may be different for your students than they are for you, and you need to discover what they are. Second, your students' families and communities may not have a long literacy history, even including their children's parents, and this needs to be taken into account. Third, some children have been exposed to more words than others by the time they start school, and this gap needs to be shrunken and eventually eliminated, with books playing a central role.

PART THREE

What to Teach

CHAPTER 9

How to Teach:
Daily, Interactively, Need-Based

Readers learn much of what they know about reading from authors (Meek, 1987); that is, through reading authors' books. But there's also much they can learn from teachers. What should we be teaching kids to help them become better readers? This is obviously the topic of countless professional books and articles, as well as college courses and professional development work. It has also been addressed in K–12 English language arts programs and curricula for generations. (For instance, every basal reader program since time immemorial has had a scope and sequence chart.) I'm not going to lay out a full scope and sequence here, but rather focus on a small number of crucial points about what teaching should look like in support of the specific goals of reading more books and reading harder books. There are many books available on each of the topics of the chapters in this section; I'm not trying to replace the detailed examples that those offer but rather to present six big ideas for framing your teaching, with a few examples for each.

These ideas will be usable within the framework of the Common Core State Standards, but the standards aren't where I'm starting from. This is good literacy curriculum no matter what, and I believe that in many ways it can not only cover what's in those standards but improve on them. I've organized these two chapters around six big ideas: daily teaching; interactive teaching; teaching based on what students need to learn; vocabulary development; getting stronger at reading both fictional and informational text; and connections to the Common Core State Standards and other big-picture frameworks. Much of the focus of these teaching ideas will be on helping students develop abilities to transition to more complex text. The guiding principles are frequency of teaching, relevance of teaching, overcoming obstacles to reading harder books, and developing more sophistication.

Teach Every Day

If kids are just reading every day, even if they're having weekly conferences with you, it's not much more than a study hall. We're also there for instruction, and instruction needs to be part of our English language arts curriculum every day. By teaching something new every day, I also mean teaching students something they don't already know. This obviously varies from student to student, but it's crucially different from following a scope and sequence[1] chart about what to teach. These charts, and the lessons they index, often feel very "technical" and are geared to general grade-level requirements, not the needs of your students.

I'd like to contrast an example of the teacher's deciding on a teaching focus for the day with a textbook-derived example. Let's say you're doing a second-grade unit of study, early in the school year, on fiction with animals in it, where you're reading some books aloud to the class. Let's say that today's is one of the *Dodsworth* series, by Tim Egan, about an animal (whose species I couldn't determine but appears mole-like) that travels to various cities and meets other animals. You've also set up a center with a variety of books about animals (fiction and informational) for children's independent reading, which some but not all of the students are reading. Early

---

[1] If you aren't familiar with the term, they're best known for their use in reading textbook series (basal readers), where they lay out the topics of every lesson in the program in a chart categorized by type of knowledge, such as phonics or comprehension, with many subcategories and connections across grade levels. Examples are easy to find online.

in the unit, you've decided to do some exploration of the literary elements of character, setting, and plot. Your students are old enough now to start thinking about how books don't just appear out of nowhere but are the result of choices that authors make, choices that we can think about as we read. As your teaching focus, you decide on "Authors decide who's in their story, where it happens, and what happens."

You begin by asking the students to say who was in today's Dodsworth book and listing the characters. You might choose to continue by asking the students to talk about which characters we get to know a little and which ones are more in the background. Then ask about where the story takes place. The books in the series are entitled *Dodsworth in [name of city]* … , so the settings are important. Then ask about what happens in the story. You could extend this by inviting students to make a simple story map with a partner, such as a numbered list of six main events. (This is richer than a simple beginning, middle, and end.) Then ask, "Who decided all these things about the story?" as a way to underline the concept of authorship. You can extend the discussion by inviting sharing about the characters, setting, and plot of animal books they're reading individually.

A follow-up lesson might focus on how animals are developed as characters in children's book; for instance, do they act like animals, or are they anthropomorphized? All of this links back to your teaching focus for the day, which in this case is part of a unit of study, but could also be a stand-alone lesson that you've decided is an age-appropriate way to take a simple look at these three literary elements. The terminology itself, which students may or may not be familiar with, can easily be introduced in the discussion. But the main point is teaching children that authors make decisions about literary elements in writing a story. It fits into a larger picture by helping students become more ready to read harder books where these elements are developed more extensively.

For contrast, I looked online for a sample lesson from a major reading series publisher and found one on "Analyze character, setting, and plot," as an example of a scope-and-sequence-driven lesson. (This one was presented as a free online supplemental lesson rather than in the core program, but is representative.) The teacher is told to review the terms *character*, *setting*, and *plot* and is given a simple story of about fifty words to write on the board and read with students. The directions then say, "Ask: Who is this story about? Where and when does the story happen? What happens in the story? Help students identify clues as necessary." Notice, most crucially, that there isn't really any thinking for children, more of a recitation of obvious answers to narrow questions; children aren't learning something they didn't know before.

So ask yourself every day, "What new idea, concept, or strategy am I teaching today?" Even if you're pulling your teaching focus from the Common Core State Standards or a scope and sequence chart, you can approach it in a way that starts from what's appropriate for your students at this point in their development. The example from the major publisher was almost certainly contracted out to a supplier who creates content targeted to a list of specifications, content that would in any case be generic rather than suited to your students.

I'd also like to underline one more important point about teaching something new every day, which is the fact of actually *teaching*. We all know that teaching in one sense encompasses everything that goes on in the classroom all day, including the physical environment, students working individually and in groups, and the teacher playing multiple roles such as coach, small-group leader, and so on. But what I'm talking about here is directly helping students acquire new knowledge. My college teacher-education students observe literacy teaching out in schools early in their program, and we talk in class about the amount and type of teaching that they see. In some cases, there's none; the teacher may direct students through a series of activities, ask them questions about a reading, and have them share what they've done, but never directly focus on the learning of something students didn't know before.

A primary-grade example of this more simplistic teaching would be reading aloud a picture book version of an Aesop's fable (perhaps with questioning like "How do you think the tortoise will do in the race?,") having them write their own fable, and then sharing the writing orally. The teacher might mention that fables always have morals so to make sure that they include one in their own fables, but without a deeper teaching of the big idea about fables, which is that they're stories (traditional and modern versions), almost always with anthropomorphized animals, that illustrate some perhaps surprising truth about human behavior. The moral serves as a charming and surprising capstone to the story. This would be true teaching, building on students' reading to help them toward a generalization that they'd be unlikely to come to on their own.

The formulaic activity described here would be enough to check off having spent time on the second-grade standard, "Recount stories, including fables and folktales from diverse cultures, and determine their central message, lesson, or moral," but only shallowly, without the powerful learning that would come from teaching kids something about what fables are really all about. Briefly, one way of teaching this would be to read two fables aloud, invite children to talk about what they have in common, and then use that to talk about the central defining characteristics of fables that I shared above. Adding in contemporary fables like those found in *Squids Will Be Squids* and Arnold Lobel's *Fables* would make the lesson even livelier. Let's move on now to our next big idea about instruction, that it should be interactive.

Teach Interactively

As I see more and more hype about putting college instruction online, I often wonder how this can even make sense. For a lecture to six hundred students, yes. But isn't teaching all about give and take, students asking the teacher questions, talking to each other, and so on? I have similar questions about online charter schools, which seem to be largely about reading, worksheets, and tests, with teachers available for phone consultation but not much else (www.nytimes.com/2011/12/13/education/online-schools-score-better-on-wall-street-than-in-classrooms.html). The joy of teaching—and its impact—are all about how it builds on the interaction with and among learners. First-grade teachers are of course not conducting lectures. But 1–12 teaching can often become didactic, in the sense of being more scripted than spontaneous. Think about a continuum from prewritten to interactive teaching. Here's an example of two lessons on the difference between fiction and nonfiction.

Think middle school, teaching about simile and metaphor. A typical (based on a common treatment of this topic), didactic, and preplanned lesson, whether in workbook or instructional form, might have as a goal "Students will be able to [SWBAT] distinguish between a metaphor and simile." It would define similes as comparisons made using *like* or *as*, and metaphors as comparisons made without those words. Typically students would be given a few examples of each, and then asked to identify several examples as one or the other, then perhaps take a quiz.

In contrast, a very interactive lesson might have the teaching goal as "Understand what similes and metaphors add to writing." You could begin by giving students a list of randomly arranged similes and metaphors. (It would be especially great if you pulled examples from books students are familiar with.) Think of Judy Blume's middle child feeling "like the peanut butter part of a sandwich," or Robert Frost's spider "holding up a moth/Like a white piece of rigid satin cloth," or Amy Lowell's "Life is a stream/On which we strew/Petal by petal the flower of our heart." Invite them to talk about the passages with a partner or in a small group, with guiding questions such as: What do all these passages have in common? Can you see a way to divide them into two different groups (although the distinction between simile and metaphor is perhaps the least important part of the lesson)? Why did the writer say it this way rather than saying "It's no fun being the middle child"? (Goodman, 1988). This could also be a whole-class discussion. Then use the students' reactions to bring out the value of figurative language; you're likely, of course, to then use the terms *simile* and *metaphor*, but they're secondary to the big idea of how writers use them to make the writing livelier and more thought-provoking. You can, as a follow-up, invite students to keep an eye out for similes and metaphors in their next couple of days of reading, and then turn that into another day's lesson, perhaps on talking about how writers sometimes use this figurative language in particularly fresh ways.

The interactive lesson is more open-ended, without a fixed sense of where it's going to end up, but this is a good thing: it goes to places that suit your students' discoveries and learning. Note that it also meets the didactic lesson's extremely modest goal, but goes so much further in helping children to understand this one aspect of complex text. (You could also, by the way, further broaden the focus by exploring how a metaphor can be much longer than a phrase; for instance, Robert Frost's "Birches" and Ted Hughes's "The Thought-Fox" are poem-length metaphors.) In your own planning for instruction, then, think about how to make your teaching more toward the interactive end of the spectrum; if you're using a curriculum that even suggests what the teacher should say, make it your own and leave room to go beyond the opening teacher moves by building on the students' responses.

Teach Kids What They Need to Learn

There are two important parts to teaching students what they need to learn, generally and in the service of being able to read harder books: first, don't teach them what they already know just because it's in the curriculum. If they're able to read books independently, they don't need lessons on digraphs anymore. Second, although you may be choosing your teaching goals in part based on a curriculum or the Common Core State Standards, think about what *you* know your students need or could benefit from. What drives you crazy? "When I'm having a conference with a kid and ask her to tell me about the book, she always does a blow-by-blow of the *entire* plot!" If this is most of your kids, try a lesson on how to do an oral précis; that is, a brief summation of a book. This could be fun to model for kids and then have them try out with a partner. What's the reason for learning how to do this (besides not driving your teacher nuts during conferences)? It's a mature way of talking to others about books. When your mom asks what the book you're reading is about, you can respond the way an adult might, "It's the story of an adolescent girl whose life is changed forever when an asteroid crashes into the moon and the whole climate changes in unpredictable ways,"[2] rather than, "They were watching the news, and the asteroid was about to hit the moon, and then it did, and nobody knew what would happen next, but they were all really scared, and she's writing about it in her diary ..." Creating an oral précis for a book is a nice ability to have, isn't it?

Another possible example: when your class visits the school library, a significant number of the students just pull books randomly off the shelves and glance through them without seeming to have more sophisticated book-finding strategies. You could perhaps have a small-group lesson, for the kids who seem to need it, or those who would just be interested in how to better use this library time to find books they'll really like. How to plan the lesson? Pretty much common sense. What do you do yourself to find a book at the library? Before you go, you might think about what you might like to look for; look back at what you've read this year to see what authors you might like to read more of; ask the librarian for tips (maybe "I liked *Speak*; can you recommend something similar?"); look up call numbers for nonfiction; look at the new arrivals section.

One more: maybe your students don't seem very strong at pulling out what's most important in informational books, focusing more on interesting tidbits than main ideas. This doesn't always matter, if you're reading the book primarily for pleasure or because you have a general interest in the topic. But if the reading is connected to a content-related unit of study or research project, readers will want to be more planful. It might make sense, for instance, if high school students are doing a term paper on a topic of their choice for a history class, for the history and English language arts teacher to collaborate in a unit of study on how to read like a researcher: evaluating the quality of sources, flagging the most important material provided by a particular book, taking notes relevant to your topic, and so on. These are the kinds of strategies found often in secondary curriculum guides; the reading part of

---

[2] Life as We Knew it (Pfeffer, 2006).

all of this is that it helps students develop the sophistication to read complex texts with a particular goal in mind, and to integrate the reading of multiple texts on the same subject. Ideally, this can be done at a time that they're actually writing a research paper. Simpler versions of these lessons will be relevant for younger students; even primary-grade students can write simple informational texts based on expertise they've gained through reading.

These are just a few examples, but the big idea is a simple one with wide application: tune in to what you're thinking your students need to get better at as readers, and teach them how to get better at it. A good way to put it into practice: at the end of the school day, think about "I noticed today that the kids [or a single student] weren't doing as well as I'd like with … ," or "today's lesson got me thinking that a good next step would be …" and try to turn it into instruction.

10

Two Ideas About What to Teach

There are obviously many, many ideas of what to teach. I'm presenting two in this chapter: first, vocabulary, since it's a powerful access tool for reading harder books; and second, learning more about the elements of both fiction and informational books, in order to increase readers' sophistication with them as they move up to harder books. This includes both being able to read harder books independently and being able to understand their complexities.

Build Vocabulary

Vocabulary development is really, really important, and so is making it a focus of the reading curriculum. A bigger vocabulary will benefit students throughout their lives, and is crucial for helping them read more complex texts. Let's start with three important things we know about vocabulary. First, we can conceptualize vocabulary as having three tiers (Beck, McKeown, and Omanson, 1987). Tier One words are used for everyday social interactions and basic reading; they include the most frequently used words in the language. These are the words that native speakers will all know by the time they start school. Tier Two words are still fairly frequent but are found more in reading and in adult conversation. Tier Three words, the biggest group (about 400,000 words, as compared to several thousand each in the other two groups), are technical and academic and don't occur as often in the language. Think of *cat*, *masterpiece*, and *isotope* as examples of each tier. These provide a useful framework for thinking about vocabulary.

Second, there are wide differences in children's vocabulary sizes. An important study (mentioned earlier; Hart and Risley, 1995), estimated the average vocabulary size of children at the age of thirty-six months in the professional, working-class, and welfare families they studied as being 1116, 749, and 525 words respectively.[1] This isn't predictive; it certainly doesn't say that you're doomed to having a small vocabulary if you're poor. But it suggests that vocabulary development should be an important curriculum focus, certainly for all students, but with special urgency for children of poverty.

Third, vocabulary, particularly beyond Tier One, develops primarily through reading. Students need to learn words that they don't hear in everyday spoken language, and reading them is more efficient than formal teaching. Nagy, Herman, and Anderson (1985) documented that not only is learning new words through reading more efficient than learning them through formal teaching, it's *ten times* as efficient. Of course, for this to happen you have to be reading books that contain words that you don't already know (though not overloaded with them), and multiple exposures to a word increase how well you know it.

How do these three central ideas fit into the teaching part of "read more books, read harder books"? First, bulking up children's vocabulary needs to be central to the reading curriculum in the early grades, especially for children of poverty. Second, realize that the majority of your students' vocabulary learning will come from their reading, and that a crucial element of this is their moving continually into more complex texts. Third, particularly for older students, teaching about vocabulary is

---

[1] This study has been criticized on a variety of dimensions; see especially Dudley-Marling and Lucas, 2009. But in my view it's solid research that needs to be taken seriously.

perhaps most valuable as a way of helping students take ownership of their own vocabulary growth, rather than teaching specific words.

First-grade classrooms should be flooded with words. Here are some ideas: get as many word books as you can find, one or two copies each of multiple titles rather than a class set of dictionaries. Bookstores and Amazon are full of appropriate books; a quick Amazon search for "my first word book" turned up over a thousand titles in the children's books category, including dictionaries, multiple books of 100 first words in other languages, and, most valuably, many books that consist of page after page of labeled pictures. These books can be introduced to students early in the school year and then placed in a center for easy access: they're great just to browse in, they support beginning reading by matching a familiar picture with its representation in print, and of course they increase vocabulary every time a student comes across a picture of something she hasn't seen before. It doesn't even matter if they can pronounce the word, seeing the word *axolotl* next to a picture of one (it's a type of salamander) will set up an association even more strongly than coming across the word in written text would. These word books are also useful for beginning spelling; you can teach children how to use both the alphabetically and topically arranged ones to find the standard spelling of a word they're wanting to write or proofread.

Students also need to learn new words beyond those that can be illustrated. Rather than gearing the vocabulary you use with them to their current word knowledge, intentionally use less familiar words; for example, you might tell them, "If you're wanting to find pictures of animals you might see at a zoo, you'll have multiple choices in our word-book center." You can download a free list of the 5,000 most common words in English[2] from a major research project that's compiled them: www.wordfrequency.info/free.asp. (The list can be converted into Excel and sorted, for instance alphabetically or by parts of speech. It took me less than two minutes to post words 4,001–5,000 into a spreadsheet and alphabetize them.) For young children, you can find words they're not likely to know starting around word 1,000, and

---

[2] For language geeks, the total 60,000-word list is available for $95 if sent to an "edu" email address. Here's a sample from the higher reaches: homie, desalinated, shell-shaped, hypostatic, pizzicato.

consciously bring a few into your speech every day. Although formally teaching vocabulary isn't an effective use of time, you can put a word of the day on the board and encourage students to find ways to use it all day.[3] Reading books aloud is also a crucial way of exposing children to words they wouldn't otherwise be picking up. The first-grade classroom can easily benefit from more than one book read aloud every day: not just a storytime, but in relation to units of study in literature as well as content areas. Some of these new words in books are likely to be defined or illustrated by the author, such as *manatee* in an aquatic life book, while others can be picked up from context.

We know that children learning to speak acquire 5–7 words a day without teaching.[4] Especially in the early grades of elementary school, we can help young learners continue the process, ideally bombarding the classroom with enough words that kids don't already know, so that they're picking them up at the high end of the normal acquisition rate. To close the gap in vocabulary size across social classes, accelerate vocabulary exposure.[5] These primary-grade strategies can in some cases continue in age-appropriate ways even through high school, where a word of the day, for instance, would still work.

As children grow older, here are a few ideas for specific teaching focuses and lessons. A crucial one is helping students have ways of dealing with unfamiliar words, especially as part of trying out slightly harder books. An especially valuable general strategy is to read ahead, then (either right away, or after you've finished a larger chunk of reading) go back and make your best guess as to what the word is likely to mean and why. If you're still unsure, use the dictionary or a device to check, see how close you got, and see if the dictionary definition makes sense. Turning this into a group lesson is especially valuable, since the teacher can scaffold kids' trying

---

[3] I have fond memories of Peewee's Playhouse, where the response to someone's saying the word of the day during the course of the show was everyone's screaming really loud.

[4] Although vocabulary acquisition is somewhat smaller for adults, it slows down in large part because we no longer come across many words we don't know.

[5] Unfortunately, some programs intended for language development of high-poverty children do just the opposite, particularly *Language for Learning* in which teachers follow scripts like holding up a picture of a pencil and saying "This is a pencil. Say pencil." This actually provides children with an impoverished language environment.

to make sense of definitions that may seem opaque given the context of the word. Two examples from sixth-graders. A girl I was working with individually read a passage that referred to a girl wanting to have some quiet time before the "avalanche of her brothers" came down the stairs. She decided it must mean something like a big commotion, and was a little puzzled when the dictionary definition referred to rocks or snow crashing down a mountain. After some discussion, it fell into place, and we were able to connect it to a previous week's discussion of metaphor. Teachable moment: a confusing dictionary definition might be because the word is being used metaphorically in your book.

Another day, I was working with a small group of students volunteering words they were unsure about. The back-cover blurb of one girl's light novel mentioned that the protagonist was being stressed by her "menopausal mother" (!). She'd looked up the word, knew from her reading so far that the mother was a little cranky, but couldn't quite make the connection. The co-ed group of kids listened very maturely as the other teacher and I explained how middle-aged women's changes in hormones can make them moody sometimes, just like kids going through puberty. Teachable moment: you might understand a word's literal meaning without knowing that it has connotations connected with it. Both of these events were part of a longer conversation I was having with these students about the middle school years being good ones to push yourself into harder reading, and that part of doing this is dealing with the vocabulary. This same idea can be used, with appropriate variations, with younger and older students.

A second teaching move is to talk with students about developing more consciousness and intentionality about their own vocabulary development. Once they're old enough, you can talk to them about the concept of three tiers of words, the importance of having a good vocabulary, and how to acquire one. There are two major ways to consciously work on developing your own vocabulary: read harder words, and seek out harder words. The meanings of the words you read will come largely from context, although you can of course choose to look them up. There are also resources for doing more focused vocabulary building. Here are two teaching ideas, suitable with adaptations for middle grades and up.

Ask students what the advantages are of knowing a lot of words and having a big vocabulary. Some examples are: being able to read harder books, knowing more names of things in the world (like my sister the birdwatcher does), seeming more mature in conversation (particularly with adults), having more ways to express yourself, and appreciating literature more. (For instance, knowing the meaning of the word *locomotion* will give you a deeper level of understanding about its meaning as the title of Jacqueline Woodson's novel.) And really, it's appropriate to say to students of any age that their current grade is a good time to focus on increasing their vocabulary. What's key in this first part of a brief lesson is developing ownership of vocabulary growth as a goal, for personal reasons. I wouldn't let the words *passing tests* cross my lips; there's no need to mention this external motivation, when the personal goal serves so well in itself as taking charge of one piece of your own maturation.

In addition to coping with new words you come across in reading, students' adopting more planful strategies can take advantage of formal vocabulary-building techniques. I provided a copy of *100 Words Every Middle Schooler Should Know* (American Heritage, 2010, one in a series) to a class of sixth-graders and suggested that a few of them browse in it and see how they liked it; it would be very easy to order several copies for a classroom and encourage all your students to work their way through it during the course of the year. This series of books, for middle school through adult, is especially good since it was published by the editors of a major dictionary, but there are comparable books for younger grades, as well as a plethora of other books for vocabulary development for those who are interested. I think it would also be fun to make students aware of the 5,000-word online list and have them come up with ideas about how to become familiar with all the words on it. It doesn't quite include all the Tier Two words in the language, and they represent frequency rather than difficulty (for instance, *subsequent* is just two steps away from *cookie*), but it's a great resource for thinking about the words of English.

Bookstores and libraries are full of vocabulary development tools for adults that you may want to get copies of for your classroom. The especially good *Merriam-Webster's Vocabulary Builder* is also available electronically, arranged in topical units; its index is also useful for students who want to find a more complex explanation of a word than a dictionary offers; for example, *pedigree* includes a brief definition, an example sentence, and a paragraph describing why the word's etymology comes from the root meaning *foot*. Students using books like these for self-directed study will be more efficient than the class studying individual words, since each student can focus on the words they want to learn and skip over the ones they already know. They also provide opportunities to pick up words kids haven't come across in reading.

Students might enjoy keeping a master list of new words as they learn them; a class can make a pact to try out their new words in conversation with each other, in part for the fun it provides. Vocabulary development is important as a tool for becoming more literate and more knowledgeable generally, and reading is also the prime avenue for making vocabulary development happen.

Fiction and Nonfiction: Getting Better at Reading Both

One more important teaching point considers the role of teaching in helping students read harder books and deal with complexity. I'm providing a few highlights for framing this teaching, rather than trying to be exhaustive. I'll discuss fiction first, then nonfiction, each with some big ideas for planning some of your teaching on them to meet the specific goal of getting better at reading them. This is above and beyond other teaching on subjects like exploring a genre, making personal connections to novels, using nonfiction as a foundation for writing research papers, and so on.

Fiction: Beyond Personal Response

In some ways, personal response is the whole point of reading fiction, particularly once you're no longer in school. Joan Lazar, a reading specialist in New Jersey, tells her middle school students that reading a novel can connect you with someone who's thinking about the same things you are, stuff that may be too personal to even share with your friends and family. For adults, fiction takes us outside of our everyday lives and gets us thinking and feeling. Personal response is often the goal and the starting point.

But Louise Rosenblatt (1995), the scholar most strongly identified with reader response theory, made it clear that literary reading involves a transaction with the text: not just the reader's reaction, not the intrinsic meaning of the text, but how the reader makes the text her own. For this to happen fully, the reader needs to be able to access the text, and understand how to return to the text to substantiate and deepen her reactions to it. If this process happens in a community of readers, all the better.

A role for instruction, therefore, can be to help readers deepen their personal responses to literature by helping them to better access an author's work. I'd like to suggest four main ways to do this: focusing on literary elements; learning to deal with longer words, sentences, chapters, and books; moving outside your comfort zone; and exploring complex and innovative narrative strategies. I'm providing some examples to help spark your own ideas for the kids and books you work with.

Literary Elements

Four major literary elements to help students explore are the old standbys: character, plot, setting, and theme. (For a much more extensive exploration of literary elements, see Lukens, Smith, and Coffel, 2012.) As I described in Chapter 9, you can talk even with young children about the choices the author has made in using these elements to construct a story. As the books they read get more sophisticated, so too can the teaching that you do, using these elements as a tool for reader response. This is often done well in the discussion of a class book. For instance, *Sarah, Plain and Tall* is memorable for its prairie setting. A lesson could consist of finding and recording the author's descriptions of the setting throughout the book, and examining how they set a mood and perhaps resonate with what's going on with the characters. A small group reading a book in common might each take a character to focus on during the reading, keeping an eye out for how we get to know the character (description, speech, actions, and so on) and then comparing notes. Plot goes well beyond identifying the beginning, middle, and end of a short piece. Making story maps of a book in a particular genre can help students better appreciate how the plot structure serves the intent of the text. For instance, in mysteries the author wants to drop hints that eventually lead to the solution of the crime without giving it away, so that at the end you can feel surprised but not cheated.

Themes are a little harder to explore because they're less obvious. Resist the urge to define a book's theme in one word ("hope"); think instead about the big ideas that a book leaves you with. ("In tough times, having just one person who believes in you can give you hope.") One way to explore themes in students' individual reading is have them use Post-its® or entries in a writing notebook when they perceive a big idea in the book, such as "being part of a community is really important" for *The Hunger Games*.

Longer

Part of increasing text complexity is that everything gets longer: words, sentences, chapters, and books. Teaching can be used to support readers' ability to handle all of these. In addition to the vocabulary development ideas I presented in the previous section of this chapter, with longer words, instruction can focus on the general challenges that long words offer us: How do you pronounce them, and is it okay to just figure out the meaning of a word and not the pronunciation? If we want to break it up into parts, how do we know where to break it up? How do we know if comparing it to another word we know will be accurate? (For instance, the first part of *helicopter* isn't related to *helium*, but the second part is related to *pterodactyl*.)

Longer (and of course more complex) sentences can be a big part of what makes harder books harder. Learning how to read them will come primarily through reading, but it's always a suitable instructional move to talk about them, whether in a reading conference, using a sentence taken from a book the class is reading together, or with general strategies, such as using the punctuation or the verbs to focus on one chunk at a time. Let's return to the long sentence from *Invisible Man* that I quoted earlier: "Upon *hearing* that one of the unemployed brothers *was* an ex-drill master from Wichita, Kansas, I *organized* a drill team of six-footers whose duty it *was* to *march* through the streets *striking* up sparks with their hob-nailed shoes." There are six verbs here in different forms, which provide a meaning structure for the sentence as a whole. Each verb can be connected to a "who" (the narrator, or the six-footers).

Longer chapters (particularly for students transitioning from easy readers to longer chapter books) and longer books are a matter of stamina. Little instruction is needed, but they're certainly worth talking about. One of my own strategies for stamina in a longer book is to read one-fifth of it at a sitting (or a smaller fraction if it's very long). If students have goals for volume of reading, number of pages is likely to be better than number of books, so that they aren't worried about falling behind because of a book's length. There is also substantial pleasure to be found from immersing yourself in a lengthy book or series, as many readers have learned from *Harry Potter* and *The Hunger Games*.

Going Outside Your Comfort Zone

Readers choose their own books, but we can nudge them. Obviously, reading more widely will develop your reading muscles for reading more widely still. Genre study is one way that the teacher can support this. If your kids haven't read plays, for instance, find some for them to read and act out (either as readers' theater or staged), exploring the unique conventions of how they're written. There are also a few screenplays of children's movies available. Graphic novels are another great genre to explore. Some teachers are afraid they're too hard for kids to read, but they're actually easier once you learn how to read them, since they have visual support just like picture books do. Students generally love them. Another form of moving beyond one's comfort zone is moving into adult books, which may begin in middle school. Teacher guidance is appropriate here, since some adult novels are fine for kids this age while others aren't. You can also make suggestions about moving beyond your comfort zone as a general lesson topic, perhaps with follow-up in individual conferences. You may have examples from your own reading to share: "I was nervous about reading a novel where a little Spanish was mixed in, but not only did I love the book, I stretched my reading muscles a little from figuring it out."[6]

Diverse Story Structure and Author's Techniques

I got this idea from David Lodge's book *The Art of Fiction*, where in fifty short, readable chapters, he explores fifty literary techniques, using a different author's work to illustrate each one.

As kids read harder fiction, they'll discover that stories aren't always constructed chronologically with a single first-person narrator; they may have flashbacks, multiple narrators (*Everything for a Dog*), multiple stories that come together at the end (*American-Born Chinese*), or cover a long period of time (*Jefferson's Sons*). Anytime you're aware of an author's doing something different, you can use it to help students understand more about how literature works. The techniques I just mentioned affect the whole structure of a book; any of them could suggest a class book where you can explore the literary technique in detail with all your students.

---

[6] I'm thinking of MacArthur Genius Award winner Junot Diaz's Pulitzer-Prize winner *The Brief Wondrous Life of Oscar Wao* (2008).

Lodge also explores devices that are less integral to a book's structure, but fun to think about: lists, the choice and use of names, a sense of how the past is different from today, point of view, telephone conversations, and many more. You could pick out the literary techniques that some of your favorite authors use, and help kids learn about and understand them. Two that strike me are Frank Cottrell Boyce's use of story premises that are just beyond real life in *Millions* and *Cosmic* and Susan Beth Pfeffer's *Last Survivors* trilogy, with different protagonists in the first two books who come together in the third, all living after an asteroid has hit the moon and caused havoc. A recent adult book, *The Age of Miracles*, is terrific in its use of the earth's slowing down as a book-length metaphor for a girl's entry into adolescence, as well as a terrific plot device. John Updike was known for his really good use of figurative language. His teenage-protagonist novel, *The Centaur*, not only revisions the Greek myth in a contemporary setting but contains sentences like this one: "The long, dim walls of the ochre hall wavered; the classroom doors, inset with square numbered panes of frosted glass, seemed experimental panels immersed in an activated liquid charged with children's voices chanting French, singing anthems, discussing problems of Social Science." Overwritten perhaps, but what fun to look at and discuss. How and why does he write like this? I'd recommend Lodge's book as a great read on its own, but you can also find plenty of material in the books your students are reading for close reading and discussion of literary devices.

Nonfiction: Working Our Way Up to the Harder Stuff

Traditionally, students have been said to learn to read and then read to learn, but contemporary literacy educators realize that it's more complex than that. As I suggest in Chapter 8, children can begin reading independently fairly early, but the process of becoming a reader doesn't end at that point; it's all about getting better at it. Also, even the youngest children are learning from what they read, and are increasingly reading nonfiction, although there comes a point at which students are expected to have reading under their belt to the point that they're presumably able to read and understand whatever's handed to them in content-area classes, although this is likely to be wishful thinking to some extent.

Another piece of the picture is the switch from a focus on reading in the early grades to a focus on literature in English language arts classes in high school; to the extent that teenagers are expected to learn about particular periods and authors, literature is the content of English language arts, while for younger students it's backgrounded. Also, in elementary school, reading in the content areas occurs in the same classroom as literature, which is no longer the case by high school and perhaps middle school. Informational text[7] has also gotten new attention because of the requirements of the Common Core State Standards that it represent an increasing percentage of what students are asked to read, particularly in the higher grades, and that reading standards be addressed in departmentalized subject-area classes as well as English language arts.

Let's focus, then, on the role of informational books in reading more and harder books, particularly what it will look like at different grade levels. There have been complaints about the Common Core State Standards' apparent reduction of fiction in schools, but remember that students' own reading can and should be whatever they want; in practice, these expectations have gone into the Standards' guidelines for publishers and refer more to what students will be required to read or taught as class texts. Also, informational text need not, and perhaps should not, refer particularly to textbooks. When you go into a library or bookstore, the shelves are full of all kinds of books outside of the fiction sections: biographies, popular science, politics, humor, cookbooks, pet care, travel, cultural studies, you name it. Even more to the point, this is true in the children's sections as well. Even those of us who are passionate about fictional literature have to realize that there are hordes of other books out there, many of them absolutely terrific.

---

[7] A term currently used rather than nonfiction, in order to identify what it is, rather than in opposition to fiction.

A major component of the role of teaching in using informational books to help students read more books and harder books is to help them learn how to read nonfiction. A good starting point is to realize that just because a book's genre is informational doesn't mean that this is your purpose for reading it. True crime is a good (lighter reading) adult example of this principle: you don't really need to know how Ted Bundy committed his murders; you read about him for — if not exactly enjoyment — a particular kind of (chilling?) reading experience. Some people read cookbooks more for pleasure than as a source of recipes that they're actually going to cook.

So perhaps a good place to start is by inviting students to read narrative nonfiction (that is, books that contain primarily text and are meant to be read from beginning to end as a whole) and explore it as a genre. (See Bomer, 2005, for a nice book-length explanation of how to do this with memoirs and memoir-type fiction written for children.) This can include picture books and graphic novels as well as text-only books, but for a unit of study on the topic I'd focus on books where any pictures are more illustrative than informational, since we're exploring narrative books before tackling more complicated formats. Examples of this: for secondary English language arts classes, the genre of literary nonfiction includes memoir, essays, and so on. For secondary content classes, many science and history books are basically narratives, such as *The Double Helix*.

The big teaching idea might be "Books don't have to be fiction to read like a story." You can have a discussion talking about how, for instance, a historical novel differs from a nonfiction account of the same time period. You don't particularly really need any new reading strategies to read narrative nonfiction, but you can use it as a basis for teaching how authors organize information, since it's different from how plot is constructed in a novel. Narrative nonfiction can engage students who don't enjoy fiction to read narrative texts (rather than just books about facts, for instance), while moving avid readers of novels into books more directly about the world.

Another important part of teaching to informational text is, of course, helping readers learn to navigate text features that are unique to these genres. An excellent unit of study (appropriate for whatever grade level you're working with, and more challenging than narrative nonfiction) can be built around the accoutrements of informational text such as table of contents, index, glossary, tables, graphs, informational photographs, labeled illustrations, timelines, maps, and so on. For younger students, even the way the words and pictures are laid out on the page may take some negotiation as to what order to read them in. In secondary grades, whatever new understanding of text features students need is likely to come in content-area classes, particularly science and mathematics.

The many professional books available on reading informational texts provide detailed ideas about how to do this. I'll provide one example. Two well-reviewed narrative-style books about Charles Darwin are *Darwin* (McGinty, 2009) and *Charles and Emma* (Heiligman, 2011). They'd be very readable for upper elementary and middle school respectively. *The Tree of Life* (Sis, 2003), with its more complex format, is a very different kind of book. Many of its pages include a chronological narrative of Darwin's life, but each page also has detailed pictures that are designed according to the information in the accompanying text. For example, one two-page spread has a cutaway diagram of the *Beagle*, the ship he traveled around the world on, plus eight small thumbnail pictures, all of it accompanied by excerpts from Darwin's shipboard journal. A fold-out page represents the main ideas of *The Origin of Species* through text and illustrations. Many teachers think that this award-winning masterpiece will be "too hard" for their students, but its Amazon editorial reviews suggest it's appropriate for fourth grade and up, and I agree; it's appropriate for upper elementary, and it provides a terrific introduction to Darwin even for adults. It's a splendid example of what teachers are for; students may not yet know how to read a book like this, and we can teach them. An ideal audience might be students who already knew something about Darwin, perhaps having read one of the narrative biographies; their knowledge of the content would be a scaffold for learning how to read the book's unusual format. The how-to would be as simple as a walk-through and a discussion about what order you might read the various chunks of text in.

Finally, learning to read informational texts well often involves making sense of them and understanding them in slightly different ways than one does with fiction. You might use shorter pieces as class texts for understanding topics like understanding the author's organization of the information, how to identify the most important ideas in what you read, how to take notes to reframe the content for yourself, and so on. The larger goal in all of this is how to teach students to get better at reading informational text so that they can read more of it on their own. This can include conversations with students about whether they're coming across any difficulties in reading nonfiction, which can then be dealt with either in conferences or lessons.

For high school and departmentalized middle schools, teaching about informational text is an excellent opportunity for collaboration across subjects; a literacy coach can be especially helpful here. I think an excellent outcome to aim for at all grade levels, and to think about in helping students set their reading goals, is for students to read a mix of fiction and nonfiction (the proportions can vary by student), and feel comfortable enough with the latter to push themselves to read harder exemplars of it, particularly on topics of interest to them. Nonfiction is a great avenue for deeper reading and learning, and you can read harder books on a topic that you have more knowledge about. Think about what kinds of informational books you'd like your students to be able to read by the end of the year, and supplement your suggesting books to them with helping them develop the muscles to read them.

The Common Core State Standards

The establishment of the Common Core State Standards for English language arts, which are for all practical purposes national standards, are likely to influence practice, in many cases dramatically, for the foreseeable future. Although the standards themselves specify what students should learn, not how that learning should be achieved, publishers have been given guidelines (www.corestandards.org/assets/Publishers_Criteria_for_3–12.pdf) for preparing aligned materials.

Curriculum publishers are, of course, likely to pay close attention to the student assessments that two state consortiums, PARCC and SBAC, are developing. States and districts are very likely to adopt published curricula in an attempt to ensure that students are meeting the standards and passing the tests. A critique of the standards and how they're likely to be carried out is beyond the scope of this book; however, it would sell your students short to have them read only what's assigned in a Core-aligned textbook and only teaching the lessons from that book. One particular concern is that those materials might focus too much on teaching lessons using texts at the prescribed level of complexity for the grade level, leaving in the dust the kids who aren't there yet.

However, it's also possible to keep a focus on reading more books and harder books while still attending to the Common Core State Standards. Here's the plan. Throughout this book, I've focused on what should be going on in your classroom on a daily basis: plenty of reading, and teaching that supports growth in reading. However, it's also useful to think about the entire year, and in doing so you can consider how to incorporate the Common Core State Standards. The standards themselves are very simple. The easiest way to find them is to Google "CCSS" or go directly to corestandards.org. Each grade level has ten reading standards for literary text and ten for informational text.[8] Grades 6–12 also have ten standards for reading in history/social studies, science, and technical subjects, which will be the responsibility of the teachers of those subjects, possibly the regular classroom teacher in middle school. Some are more elaborate than others, but there aren't very many standards. There are also lists of texts for each grade range, but these are examples of complexity, not required readings.

Here's my three-part plan for incorporating the standards into your literacy program. First, find all the relevant standards for your grade level and print them out. If you haven't looked at them already, you're likely to be reassured by how

---

[8] There are also foundational skills for reading in grades K-5; these are largely technical aspects of reading acquisition, such as reading words with suffixes, that need little formal teaching.

reasonable and manageable they are; they do indeed provide a good list of topics to teach. Second, think about whether there are some that could be the basis for an entire unit of study and others that lend themselves to briefer teaching. For instance, the seventh fourth-grade standard for informational text asks students to interpret information that's presented other than by narrative text, as in graphs and timelines. You might find it useful to present a unit where students learn to really drill down on reading these kinds of text features. Better yet, you might do so in the context of a history unit, where students are using a variety of texts to learn, for instance, about the history and geography of their state. The state would be the content focus of the unit, and non-narrative text features would be the literacy focus of the unit. The second fourth-grade standard for literary text, however, is to determine the theme of a short work of literature and summarize it. This is a much more general standard that should be addressed frequently throughout the year.

Similarly, high school students are asked to compare works of literature to their presentation in various other media, such as film and performance, which could encompass an entire unit of study, or be a segment of topical units (listening to recorded poems; attending a theatrical performance). Analyzing the structure of an argument in an informational text at that grade level, however, is a smaller piece of teaching, and might well be integrated into a unit of study on writing such text.

Third, as you think about your curriculum for the year, use the Common Core State Standards for your grade level as one tool for thinking about what to include. Notice that I've said *one* tool; the standards don't need to be the basis of your entire curriculum. Also, the standards documents themselves say very explicitly that they don't prescribe how teachers should achieve them. For an example of one way to approach them through literature-based units of study, go to commoncore.org/maps. (They no longer have free samples, but you can access all their content with a twenty-dollar membership or buy the materials in book form.) There are enough activities provided that you can pick and choose, and all the standards are addressed over the course of each year's six units of study. They can also, of course, give you ideas for developing your own units of study. They're an especially useful resource for new teachers.

Arthur Applebee, a long-term scholar and professor of English language arts education, and part of the Common Core State Standards development team, has suggested (personal communication, 2011) that teachers background the standards; that is, address them without making them into the curriculum itself. The idea behind them is that students will achieve them, not that they're the extent of what students will learn. I strongly endorse Applebee's perspective, and would like to add two provisos for teachers to think about. First, your school may at some point purchase a textbook series tied to the standards and require you to use it. (Of course, anything you can do proactively to demonstrate that you're already making sure students meet the standards could help head this off.) Also, it's not a given that you go through a textbook in order, and you can use it as a supplement to your own broader and more comprehensive curriculum, using any teaching ideas that seem good to you, treating workbook pages as quick assessment tools, and the student anthology as just one source of reading material in the classroom. (The latter will almost certainly be too short to provide students with enough to read during the course of the year.)

The second proviso is to pay serious attention to the text complexity requirements of the standards as they continue to be further defined. Reading harder books is of course one of the major thrusts of this book, and a crucial goal for our students. It will serve teachers well to get students reading the books that are just right for them, and moving toward and into more challenging books through their own choices as well as appropriate instruction, documenting their growth throughout the year. But published curriculum materials and especially the tests are likely to emphasize what the standards have referred to as grade-level appropriate text. Students are unlikely to be able to successfully answer such test questions (and, more importantly, really be able to read complex texts) if their curriculum has been focused on close reading of grade-level texts rather than extensive reading of texts beginning where they are and gradually working up to the Common Core State Standards' version of grade level.

So Should We Have a Master List?

Not really. You need to have students reading as much as possible in increasingly harder books. You need to have individual conferences with them, where some teaching takes place. You need to teach them something new every day, as described in the last two chapters. You can include the Common Core State Standards for your grade level as part of this. I'd recommend spending time on literary topics (genres, structure and style, interpretation), informational text features and strategies, and reading strategies generally. You need to make sure that kids understand what they're reading, but this isn't achieved through covering comprehension "skills" like story sequence but rather through reading and discussion where the focus is on meaning and how it's created. A student who can't talk about what she's read needs to be helped generally, often with some scaffolding, to create meaning from text.

However, that doesn't mean there aren't good ideas out there about English language arts curriculum. But rather than a scope and sequence chart, I think teachers are best served by just reading good professional books. The best three sources, in my opinion, are Heinemann, Stenhouse, and NCTE, all with online bookstores. I also think units of study, examples of which have been developed by Lucy Calkins and many others (as well as the Common Core Curriculum Maps mentioned earlier), are a great tool for planning. Units can have a literature focus (poetry), a reading improvement and appreciation focus (following nonlinear chronology), or a content-area focus (biographies of scientists). I sometimes suggest to teachers that they may have a special interest that they can devote time to in their curriculum, so that students will be able to look back and say, for instance, "Seventh grade was the year I really learned to love and understand poetry." Also, if you personally can't tolerate reading the fantasy genre, you don't need to do a unit of study on it; kids can read it on their own and learn more about it another year. If you're a new teacher and aren't sure how you're going to fill up those 180 days of the school year, I'd buy a few professional books that have a lot of specific ideas for lessons and units of study, but you can also have a solid program just with daily reading, conferences, and teaching something new every day.

PART FOUR

What to Document

11

Knowing What and How They've Read

I've intentionally chosen to use the word *documentation* rather than *assessment* here, because assessment is a complex process that's grounded in a continual monitoring of student learning and has been written about at great length elsewhere (sometimes, it seems, ad nauseam). My focus here is narrower: to document accomplishments and growth as students read more books and harder books. Think of it as comparable to a chart where parents mark a child's height on every birthday, but with lots more detail, or the way a runner might keep a record of his mileage and speed. This documentation will help the teacher assess what support students need from the teacher and also provide evidence for others such as parents and administrators.

Documenting Volume of Reading

This is a simple record of the books students have read. I believe that librarything. com is in many ways the best tool for compiling this information, with students each having their own librarything.com account (probably with the understanding that you'll have access to it). One of the pieces of information that it can display is publishing information, including the number of pages in each book, and libraries can be sorted by the date the book was added. You might want to have each student do a monthly printout. (The information can be uploaded to a spreadsheet to print it out using less paper.) If LibraryThing doesn't work for you, a paper list, a reader's notebook, a spreadsheet, or a database can also work.

You want to be very careful not to make a big deal out of how many books or pages students are reading. Reading goals can and should be discussed as a class, but each student's goals and progress should be kept private for discussion in conferences. You also want to be sure to avoid "incentives" like wall charts of how much students have read, or stickers or other rewards. One of the best-established research findings of social psychology is that rewards tend to diminish interest in doing an activity for its own sake (Kohn, 1993). Rewards can also, of course, encourage cheating. Students might personally delight in seeing how much they've read, which is fine, but teachers shouldn't emphasize it. This is purely documentation.

Students will be reading in and outside of school, and their documentation will be most valuable if it includes everything in book form that they read. That is, books read on electronic platforms count, but not other online reading, not because it doesn't matter but because books provide more sustained acts of reading. Magazines, blogs, Facebook, and so on all involve reading, but the real reading stamina and growth come from books, which is the reading that we want to keep track of. In departmentalized secondary schools, the English language arts teacher may want to ask students to include the books (other than textbooks) that they've read for their content-area classes as well, particularly if those teachers are providing topical book lists or otherwise incorporating individual reading into the curriculum.

The amount that students are reading should also be documented by student reflection on the topic, in both conferences and written responses. Choose a week, perhaps periodically, to have every student's reading record in front of you at that week's conference and talk about how much they're reading. If they're happy with the amount, you can talk about how they're progressing on their goals generally, whether they're able to read more than they used to, any barriers they have to reading more, and so on. A written reflection, which can be as simple as responding to prompts on these topics, provides you with information that can be looked at over the course of the year. Remember that students should never be compared to others on this, only to their own goals.

Documenting Growth in Reading Ability

Your record of what students have read will also be a record of their growing ability to read harder books. Measures of text complexity are inexact, and the books readers choose vary from day to day in how hard they are, but you should be expecting to see a gradual increase in the proportion of harder books that students read. Particularly for younger children, it will often be obvious from their lists of the books that they've read, since their growth should be rapid, and using Leveled Book levels adds more precision. Remember that readers shouldn't be expected to move out of one level and never look back; readers should be choosing books on the basis of their interest in them, while being encouraged to gradually push into harder ones. As long as you're touching base with students through conferences and know that they're understanding harder books as they move into them, you know that their ability is growing.

You can also, of course, conduct an occasional informal reading inventory (Roe, 2010) if you want more formal documentation, particularly if you want to be able to quantify how many grade levels students have improved. I hesitate a little in mentioning this, since the concept of grade level in reading is very problematic in its definition and use. Saying that a student reads "at" a particular grade level just means that their score on a test is equivalent to that of the average student at that grade level taking the test. However, an informal reading inventory can compare students' reading of texts with different readability levels as defined by a standard formula; the teacher can then say that at the beginning of the year he could read only a text at a 3.2 level with good accuracy and understanding, while at the end of the year he could read a 4.7. The number isn't particularly scientific or precise, but it's not meaningless either, particularly as a comparison to the beginning-of-year number. It can also be useful if your instincts about what a particular student is able to read are a little uncertain. I'd just be careful not to say, however, that the student has made 1.5 years' progress. This would be unfounded. And beware of using IRI's or running records for inappropriate purposes, such as limiting what students are allowed to read.

Other markers of growth in reading ability are an expanding range of text types and movement toward reading longer books, both of these indicating improved reading ability. (Students will of course read books of different lengths, but you'll hope to see the emergence of longer books as the year goes forward.)

Here's a simple questionnaire for students, at least through middle school:

In the last month or so, I think I've been:

_____ reading harder books

_____ moving into longer books

_____ trying new genres (Examples: _____)

One way I think I've been getting better as a reader is:

_____

The topics on the questionnaire could then be brought up in conferences and as a class lesson, so that you're not only documenting growth in reading but involving students in reflection on it.

Just as with documentation of how much students read, documentation of how well they read is relatively simple, coming primarily through record keeping. It's crucial, however, in both cases, that the records be triangulated and confirmed by your conferences with students. Students who have problems with reading or don't like reading may try to cover up by faking their reading lists. The only real way to deal with this is to talk about the books they've recorded as having read, and respond to any suspected cheating with a conversation beginning with words like, "You don't seem to be remembering much about that book; did you have trouble getting into it?" and proceed nonpunitively with an exploration about how the *only* purpose of all this reading is to read and understand books that engage and interest them. The classroom climate also needs to be one where students understand that if they're not reading as much as they could be, they need to come to you for suggestions, inspiration, and help. They won't get into trouble by being honest; indeed, it's the teacher's job to help them to want to read.

Documenting Growth in Reading Sophistication

If students are reading harder books, much of their reading sophistication will develop on its own, but good, focused teaching can accelerate and deepen it, as discussed in Part 3. Sophistication means not just reading a book but being able to talk and write about it intelligently. For documentation, keeping a record of any assessment you did connected with your teaching will be useful. For instance, if very young children draw pictures of the events in a story and other responses to lessons, you could either keep or scan the pictures. Then create an ongoing chart that tracks, using whatever system works for you, your assessment of their understanding of the concept (as simple as a 0–3 scale), of their representation of characters, events, chronology, and so on. This can then be used for focusing what you do in future conferences and lessons.

You can document also by focusing on the Common Core State Standards for your grade level. Picking at random a section of one for seventh grade: "Analyze how a drama's or poem's form or structure (e.g., soliloquy, sonnet) contributes to its meaning." As part of a poetry unit at this grade level, I might use Paul Janeczko's terrific book *A Kick in the Head*, which is made up of descriptions and examples of twenty-nine poetic forms, including rare ones like the clerihew, and talk with students about why a poet would choose a specific form, particularly a highly constrained one like the sonnet, and the effect it has on the reader. As one activity during the unit, you could ask students to pick a poem of their choice to write about, talking about its form as one aspect of it. (Note that the standard gives *examples* of structures, not required ones, so students could write about a limerick.)

Their writing would serve as documentation of their level of sophistication about this topic, as well as exemplars of the level of analysis that can reasonably be expected of seventh-graders, given good teaching. It won't be the same as what a literary critic could do, but they could reasonably talk about how the form of a sonnet ideally presents a relatively small idea with a workable and pleasing rhythm, length, and rhyme scheme, often with a slight twist in the theme in the second stanza. The broader idea contained in the standard could also be explored by looking at chapter structure and titles in novels, the chronology of short stories, or the scenes in plays. The key in connecting to the standards specifically is being able to document that you've provided students with opportunities for meeting them, and in many cases documented the results. You won't, of course, be saving copies of all student work, but a representative sample for each standard for your grade level couldn't hurt, along with a running list of when standards have been addressed in your teaching. (Remember, again, that they aren't necessarily the heart or totality of your teaching, but you can certainly document that you're addressing them and students are meeting them.)

Documenting Identity as a Reader

Since part of the goal of reading more books and reading harder books is for students to carry an identity as a reader into adult life, providing them with opportunities to think about who they are as readers during the course of the year can be a valuable teaching move and also worth documenting. (I suggested this in Chapter 5 for the beginning of the year specifically.) This is a small piece of documentation but well worth doing. In combination with teaching and conferences, you can invite students to write, either in response to prompts or open-endedly, their thoughts about questions like these:

1. What are a few words you'd use to describe yourself as a reader?
2. How does reading rank in the ways you like to spend free time?
3. When and where do you especially like to read? Sitting or lying down; hard chair or somewhere soft; daytime or evening; a quiet space, a lively one, or with music?
4. What are some characteristics of the books you like? Short or long, similar or varied, serious or funny, fiction or informational, easy or challenging, make you think or make you feel?
5. What stand out as your favorite books and why? What wouldn't you want to be required to read?
6. How are you different as a reader than you were a year ago? What do you think your reading will be like as an adult?

This is, of course, just a starter list. These are obviously valuable as teaching and discussion topics, but I'm suggesting taking it a step further and using them as documentation so that the students and you can look back at the end of the year and see how their reading identity has developed. At the end of the school year, I'd invite them to talk and write about who they'll be as a reader over the summer; maybe take what they've written home with them as a reminder, while you save a copy to give to their next year's teacher.

Dealing with Standardized Tests

Although this chapter has focused on documentation rather than all kinds of assessment, standardized tests are of course on everyone's mind and need to be addressed. Although many state tests are still in place as I write this, I'm going to talk about the new Common Core State Standards tests that are being developed, based on the information at the time of this writing from the two consortia developing the tests, PARCC and SBAC. (Both have extensive websites; each has about half of American states as members.) It appears that they're likely to be similar to traditional tests in some ways, but to have more performance-based test items, such as writing in response to a text rather than just answering comprehension questions. The specifications for writing test items that I found at SBAC tied them very closely to the content of the standards, as did the sample test items I found at PARCC. Students are, for instance, asked to identify where evidence for a particular conclusion is found in a passage, or to read a short piece of informational text and then use the Internet to research a related topic and then write about it.

There are many concerns about these assessments. (I'm wondering, for instance, how they'll determine what level of response is appropriate for each grade level in rubric-assessed tasks.) There will certainly be attempts to teach to the tests, whether it's called that or not. Publishers are likely to produce materials with activities that look very much like the test items. But if your students are reading more books and harder books, they'll be working toward or beyond experiences with the kinds of texts that they'll be asked to respond to on the tests, since the standards explicitly refer to "grade-level complexity."

Not all of your students will get that far in what they're able to read (indeed, the standards are unrealistic and unfair if asking that all students must), but if they're starting the year with what they're able to read and making progress throughout the year, they'll be better off than in a curriculum that uses material that's too hard for them from the start. Since many of the test items are likely to involve writing in response to what they've read, they'll also need a good writing curriculum. Writing that grows out of and relates to what you're reading is, of course, important and valuable, and will fit in well with the ideas in this book about units of study and teaching every day. It's impossible to predict how schools in general will fare with this new generation of tests, and teachers are understandably upset about having their own evaluations potentially being linked to student test scores. However, it's no accident that students in wealthier communities always score better on all kinds of standardized tests. Why? Because they're reading more. Students who read more score higher on reading tests, students with more access to books and encouragement of reading read more, and students from wealthier communities have more access to books in and out of school. If students are reading enough, and ramping up what they read, and talking and writing about what they read, the tests should largely take care of themselves. Don't ignore them, but don't foreground them.

Closing Words

Imagine running into one of your students as an adult. Will she be carrying a book (paper or electronic)? Will he have a job that suits him, one that being a serious reader has helped prepare him for? Will she ask you what you've been reading lately and what you'd recommend? Will he tell you how much his own children love reading? Will she find you on social media to tell you how glad she is about all the reading she did in your class? Think about it, and start tomorrow.

Students' Guide to the Dewey Decimal System

Most public libraries use the Dewey Decimal System for nonfiction books. The numbers range from 001 to 999. Decimals after the main number are used for subcategories.

Biographies are usually in their own section, with the call number B, and arranged alphabetically by the last name of the subject of the biography.

These are the ten main categories:

000 Computer science, information & general works

100 Philosophy & psychology

200 Religion

300 Social sciences

400 Language

500 Science

600 Technology

700 Arts & recreation

800 Literature

900 History & geography

The list below is a browsing guide. It includes topics that might be interesting to students and allows them to quickly find the right section of the library to find books on a topic. When a number ends with zero, it applies to a whole section. For instance, the number 330 for money and economics means that you'll find books on the topic within call numbers 330–339. Of course, this is only a small fraction of the topics you'll find in library books!

001.9 Superstitions, aliens, monsters, and other weird stuff

004 Computers

082 Quotations

220 The Bible

230 Christianity

296 Judaism

297 Islam

300 People around the world

323 Civil rights

330 Money and economics

340 Laws

355–9 Military

363 How people help Planet Earth

371 Schools

385–388 Transportation (trains, boats, planes, spaceships, cars, and trucks)

391 Fashion

393 Mummies

394 Holidays

395 Manners

419 Sign language

423 English dictionaries

428 Fun information about language

507 Science projects and experiments

520 Astronomy (planets, galaxies, the universe)

537 Electricity

538 Magnets

550 Geology (earthquakes, volcanoes, glaciers, oceans, weather)

560 Dinosaurs and fossils

576 Evolution

577 Ecology and habitats

580 Plants

590 Animals

   597.3 Sharks

   597.9 Snakes, reptiles

   599.5 Whales and dolphins

   599.61 Elephants

   599.7 Cats, big and small, dogs, bears

616 Diseases

641 Food and cooking

736.98 Origami

741.5 Comics

745 Crafts

780 Music

792–3 Dance

796 Sports

811 Poetry

818.6 Joke books

910 Geography and travel; each continent has its own call number

   910.452 Titanic

912 Atlases and maps

919.8 Antarctica

930 History of the ancient world

940–999 History; each country or area has its own call number

   970 Native Americans

   973.7 Civil War

   973.931 American history in the 21st century

   996 Pacific Ocean islands

   998 North and South Poles

   999 Extraterrestial worlds

Bibliography

Allington, Richard L. 1977. "If They Don't Read Much, How They Ever Gonna Get Good?" *Journal of Reading* 21: 57–61.

———. 2002. *Big Brother and the National Reading Curriculum: How Ideology Trumped Evidence.* Portsmouth, NH: Heinemann.

———. 2009. *What Really Matters in Response to Intervention: Research-Based Designs.* Boston: Pearson.

———. 2012. *What Really Matters for Struggling Readers: Designing Research-Based Programs.* 3rd ed. Boston: Pearson.

Allington, R. L., and R. E. Gabriel. 2012. "Every Child, Every Day." *Reading* 69, no. 6.

Allington, R. L., and A. McGill-Franzen. 2012. Closing the Reading Achievement Gap. High-Expectation Curricula: Helping All Students Succeed with Powerful Learning. In Curt Dudley-Marling and Sarah Michaels, *High-Expectation Curricula: Helping All Students Succeed with Powerful Learning.* New York: Teachers College. 189–202.

Anderson, Richard C., Paul T. Wilson, and Linda G. Fielding. 1988. "Growth in Reading and How Children Spend Their Time Outside of School." *Reading Research Quarterly* 23: 285–303.

Appleman, Deborah. 2006. *Reading for Themselves: How to Transform Adolescents into Lifelong Readers Through Out-of-Class Book Clubs.* Portsmouth, NH: Heinemann.

Atwell, Nancie. 1998. *In the Middle: New Understandings About Writing, Reading, and Learning.* 2nd ed. Portsmouth, NH: Boynton/Cook.

Baghban, Marcia. 1984. *Our Daughter Learns to Read and Write: A Case Study from Birth to Three.* Newark, DE: International Reading Association.

Beck, I. L., M. G. McKeown, and R. C. Omanson. 1987. "The Effects and Uses of Diverse Vocabulary Instructional Techniques." In Margaret G. McKeown and Mary E. Curtis. *The Nature of Vocabulary Acquisition.* Hillsdale, NJ: Lawrence Erlbaum, 147–63.

Bedford, April Whatley, and Lettie K. Albright. 2011. *A Master Class in Children's Literature: Trends and Issues in an Evolving Field.* Urbana, IL: NCTE.

Bomer, Katherine. 2005. *Writing a Life: Teaching Memoir to Sharpen Insight, Shape Meaning— and Triumph over Tests.* Portsmouth, NH: Heinemann.

Calkins, Lucy. 1986. *The Art of Teaching Writing.* 1st ed. Portsmouth, NH: Heinemann.

Cary, Stephen. 2007. *Working with English Language Learners: Answers to Teachers' Top Ten Questions.* 2nd ed. Portsmouth, NH: Heinemann.

Clay, Marie M. 1993. *Reading Recovery: A Guidebook for Teachers in Training.* Portsmouth, NH: Heinemann.

DeFord, Diane E. 1981. "Literacy: Reading, Writing and Other Essentials." *Language Arts* 58: 52–58.

Dudley-Marling, C., and K. Lucas. 2009. "Pathologizing the Language and Culture of Poor Children." *Language Arts* 86: 362–70.

Ehrlich, Hannah. 2011. "Publishing with a Mission: Culturally Diverse Books for Children." *School Talk* 16, no. 4: 3–4.

Fountas, Irene C., and Gay S. Pinnell. 1996. *Guided Reading: Good First Teaching for All Children.* Portsmouth, NH: Heinemann.

———. 2006. *Leveled Books (K–8): Matching Texts to Readers for Effective Teaching.* Portsmouth, NH: Heinemann.

Freire, Paulo. 1970. *Pedagogy of the Oppressed* [Pedagogía del oprimido]. New York: Herder & Herder.

Gladwell, Malcolm. 2008. *Outliers: The Story of Success.* New York: Little, Brown.

Goodman, K. S. 1988. "Look What They've Done to Judy Blume!: The 'Basalization' of Children's Literature." *New Advocate* 1: 29–41.

Goodman, Yetta M. 1996. "The Roots of Literacy." In Goodman, Yetta M., and Wilde, Sandra. *Notes from a Kidwatcher: Selected Writings of Yetta M. Goodman.* Portsmouth, NH: Heinemann.

Goodman, Yetta M., and Sandra Wilde. 1996. *Notes from a Kidwatcher: Selected Writings of Yetta M. Goodman.* Portsmouth, NH: Heinemann.

Graves, Donald H. 1983. *Writing: Teachers and Children at Work.* Exeter, NH: Heinemann.

Harste, Jerome C., Virginia A. Woodward, and Carolyn L. Burke. 1984. *Language Stories and Literacy Lessons.* Portsmouth, NH: Heinemann Educational Books.

Hart, Betty, and Todd R. Risley. 1995. *Meaningful Differences in the Everyday Experience of Young American Children.* Baltimore: P. H. Brookes.

Heath, Shirley B. 1983. *Ways with Words: Language, Life, and Work in Communities and Classrooms.* New York: Cambridge University Press.

Hirsch, E. D. 1987. *Cultural Literacy: What Every American Needs to Know.* Boston: Houghton Mifflin.

Kohn, Alfie. 1993. *Punished by Rewards: The Trouble with Gold Stars, Incentive Plans, A's, Praise, and Other Bribes.* Boston: Houghton Mifflin.

Krashen, Stephen D. 2004. *The Power of Reading: Insights from the Research.* 2nd ed. Portsmouth, NH: Heinemann.

Lee, Dorris M., Roach Van Allen, and Lillian A. Lamoreaux. 1963. *Learning to Read Through Experience.* 2nd ed. New York: Appleton-Century-Crofts.

Lehman, Barbara A., Evelyn B. Freeman, and Patricia L. Scharer. 2010. *Reading Globally, K–8: Connecting Students to the World Through Literature.* Thousand Oaks, CA: Corwin Press.

Lodge, David. 1992. *The Art of Fiction.* New York: Penguin.

Lukens, Rebecca J., Jacquelin J. Smith, and Cynthia Miller Coffel. 2012. *A Critical Handbook of Children's Literature.* 9th ed. Upper Saddle River, NJ: Pearson.

Lynch-Brown, Carol, Carl M. Tomlinson, and Kathy G. Short. 2011. *Essentials of Children's Literature.* 7th ed. Boston: Pearson/Allyn.

McCracken, Robert A., and Marlene J. McCracken. 1978. "Modeling Is the Key to Sustained Silent Reading." *The Reading Teacher* 31, no. 4: 406–8.

McGee, L. M., and D. J. Richgels. 1989. "'K Is Kristen's': Learning the Alphabet from a Child's Perspective." *The Reading Teacher* 43: 216–25.

McQuillan, Jeff. 1998. *The Literacy Crisis: False Claims, Real Solutions.* Portsmouth, NH: Heinemann.

Meek, Margaret. 1987. *How Texts Teach What Readers Learn.* Stroud, UK: Thimble.

Mooney, Margaret E. 1990. *Reading to, with, and by Children.* Katonah, NY: R. C. Owen Publishers.

Moustafa, Margaret. 1997. *Beyond Traditional Phonics: Research Discoveries and Reading Instruction.* Portsmouth, NH: Heinemann.

Nagy, William E., Patricia A. Herman, and Richard C. Anderson. 1985. "Learning Words from Context." *Reading Research Quarterly* 20: 233–53.

National Endowment for the Arts. 2007. *To Read or Not to Read: A Question of National Consequence.* Washington, DC: National Endowment for the Arts. (Available at http://www.nea.gov/research/ToRead.pdf).

Parsons, Stephanie. 2010. *First Grade Readers: Units of Study to Help Children See Themselves as Readers and Meaning Makers.* Portsmouth, NH: Heinemann.

Pearson, P. D., and G. Gallagher. 1983. "The Gradual Release of Responsibility Model of Instruction." *Contemporary Educational Psychology* 8: 112–23.

Purcell-Gates, Victoria. 1995. *Other People's Words: The Cycle of Low Literacy.* Cambridge, MA: Harvard University Press.

Rhodes, Lynn K. 1993. *Literacy Assessment: A Handbook of Instruments.* Portsmouth, NH: Heinemann.

Roe, Betty D. 2010. *Informal Reading Inventory: Preprimer to Twelfth Grade.* 8th ed. Belmont, CA: Cengage Learning Wadsworth.

Rosenblatt, Louise M. 1995. *Literature as Exploration.* 5th ed. New York: Modern Language Association of America.

Ross, Catherine S. 1995. "'If They Read Nancy Drew, So What?': Series Book Readers Talk Back." *Library and Information Science Research* 17: 201–36.

Serafini, Frank. 2001. *The Reading Workshop: Creating Space for Readers.* Portsmouth, NH: Heinemann.

———. 2010. *Classroom Reading Assessments: More Efficient Ways to View and Evaluate Your Readers.* Portsmouth, NH: Heinemann.

Shannon, Patrick, and Kenneth S. Goodman. 1988. *Report Card on Basal Readers.* Katonah, NY: Richard C. Owen.

Short, Kathy G., Jerome C. Harste, and Carolyn L. Burke. 1996. *Creating Classrooms for Authors and Inquirers.* 2nd ed. Portsmouth, NH: Heinemann.

Smith, Michael W., and Jeffrey D. Wilhelm. 2002. *Reading Don't Fix No Chevys: Literacy in the Lives of Young Men.* Portsmouth, NH: Heinemann.

Stotsky, Sandra. 2012. *The Death and Resurrection of a Coherent Literature Curriculum: What Secondary English Teachers Can Do.* Lanham, MD: Rowman & Littlefield.

Taberski, Sharon. 2000. *On Solid Ground: Strategies for Teaching Reading K–3.* Portsmouth, NH: Heinemann.

Tomlinson, Carl M., and Carol Lynch-Brown. 2010. *Essentials of Young Adult Literature.* 2nd ed. Boston: Pearson.

Veatch, Jeannette, and Warren Goodrich. 1964. *How to Teach Reading with Children's Books.* New York: Teachers College, Bureau of Publications.

Veatch, Jeannette. 1978. *Reading in the Elementary School.* 2nd ed. New York: Wiley.

Wilde, Sandra. 1992. *You kan red this!: Spelling and punctuation for whole language classrooms, K-6.* Portsmouth, NH: Heinemann.

———. 1997. *What's a Schwa Sound Anyway?: A Holistic Guide to Phonetics, Phonics, and Spelling.* Portsmouth, NH: Heinemann.